Teaching Grammar, Structure

Teaching Grammar, Structure and Meaning introduces teachers to some basic ideas from the increasingly popular field of cognitive linguistics as a way of explaining and teaching important grammatical concepts. Particularly suitable for those teaching post-16 English Language, this book offers a methodology for teaching major aspects of linguistic form and an extensive set of learning activities. Written by an experienced linguist and teacher, this book contains:

- an evaluation of current approaches to the teaching of grammar and linguistic form;
- a revised pedagogy based on principles from cognitive science and cognitive linguistics;
- a comprehensive set of activities and resources to support the teaching of the main linguistic topics and text types;
- a detailed set of suggestions for further reading and a guide to available resources.

Arguing for the use of drama, role play, gesture, energy dynamics and visual and spatial representations as ways of enabling students to understand grammatical features, this book explores and analyses language use in a range of text types, genres and contexts. This innovative approach to teaching aspects of grammar is aimed at English teachers, student teachers and teacher trainers.

Marcello Giovanelli is Lecturer in English in Education at the University of Nottingham, UK.

NATE

The National Association for the Teaching of English (NATE), founded in 1963, is the professional body for all teachers of English from primary to post-16. Through its regions, committees and conferences, the association draws on the work of classroom practitioners, advisers, consultants, teacher trainers, academics and researchers to promote dynamic and progressive approaches to the subject by means of debate, training and publications. NATE is a charity reliant on membership subscriptions. If you teach English in any capacity, please visit **www.nate.org.uk** and consider joining NATE, so the association can continue its work and give teachers of English and the subject a strong voice nationally.

This series of books co-published with NATE reflects the organisation's dedication to promoting standards of excellence in the teaching of English, from early years through to university level. Titles in this series promote innovative and original ideas that have practical classroom outcomes and support teachers' own professional development.

Books in the NATE series include both pupil and classroom resources and academic research aimed at English teachers, students on PGCE/ITT courses and NQTs.

Titles in this series include:

International Perspectives on Teaching English in a Globalised World
Andrew Goodwyn, Louann Reid and Cal Durrant

Teaching English Language 16–19
Martin Illingworth and Nick Hall

Unlocking Poetry (CD-ROM)
Trevor Millum and Chris Warren

Teaching English Literature 16–19
Carol Atherton, Andrew Green and Gary Snapper

Teaching Caribbean Poetry
Beverley Bryan and Morag Styles

Sharing not Staring: 25 Interactive Whiteboard Lessons for the English Classroom, 2nd Edition
Trevor Millum and Chris Warren

Teaching Grammar, Structure and Meaning

Exploring theory and practice for post-16
English Language teachers

Marcello Giovanelli

LONDON AND NEW YORK

First published 2015
by Routledge
2 Park Square, Milton Park, Abingdon, Oxon OX14 4RN

and by Routledge
711 Third Avenue, New York, NY 10017

Routledge is an imprint of the Taylor & Francis Group, an informa business

British Library Cataloguing in Publication Data
A catalogue record for this book is available from the British Library

Library of Congress Cataloging in Publication Data
Giovanelli, Marcello.
Teaching grammar, structure and meaning : exploring theory and practice for post-16 English language teachers / Marcello Giovanelli.
pages cm — (National association for the teaching of english (nate))
1. English language—Grammar—Study and teaching (Secondary) 2. Cognitive grammar. I. Title.
LB1631.G53 2014
428.0071'2—dc23
2014005491

ISBN: 978-0-415-70987-3 (hbk)
ISBN: 978-0-415-70988-0 (pbk)
ISBN: 978-1-315-76202-9 (ebk)

Typeset in Galliard
by FiSH Books Ltd, Enfield

MIX
Paper from
responsible sources
FSC
www.fsc.org FSC® C013056

Printed and bound in Great Britain by
TJ International Ltd, Padstow, Cornwall

Contents

List of illustrations

Figures

Tables

Acknowledgements

This book would not have been possible without the encouragement and help of many people. I am grateful to the following for their support in either sharing ideas, providing advice and suggestions, pointing me in the way of extra reading, answering queries or providing assistance with photographs and other technical aspects: Fay Banks, Barbara Bleiman, Ron Carter, Billy Clark, Dan Clayton, Charlotte Coleman, Oliver Conopo, Phil de Jager, Lydia Dunkley, Sadie Ellis, Anton Franks, Dora Giovanelli, Angela Goddard, Molly Gray, Jessie Hillery, Dick Hudson, Kate Hughes, Phil Kelly, Kristina Lawson, Steve Nikols, Steve Phillips, Peter Stockwell and Felicity Titjen. I would also like to thank Sarah Tuckwell and Alison Foyle at Taylor and Francis for their support at various stages of the writing, and Anne Fairhall for her assistance and guidance when this book was at the early proposal stage.

Dan Clayton, Cathy Eldridge, Louise Greenwood, Lacey McGurk and Jess Mason all provided constructive feedback on early versions of the manuscript. I am most grateful for their careful reading, and their sound advice and insightful suggestions.

I would also like to thank participants at a workshop I ran on grammar and embodied learning at the 2012 conference of the National Association for the Teaching of English (NATE) in York for their enthusiasm for, and feedback on, a number of ideas that have ended up in this book. Many of the activities have also been used with students at The Duston School, Northampton, Higham Lane School, Nuneaton, and in both the School of English and the School of Education at the University of Nottingham. I am grateful to these students for all they have taught me about the best ways to study language.

My wife Jennie read and commented wisely on various drafts of the book and offered her love and support throughout the writing period. She and our daughters, Anna, Zara and Sophia, deserve my biggest thanks of all.

I am grateful to the following for permission to reproduce material: Brad McCain for the *Internet Marketing* advertisement, The British Library for an extract from its 'Conditions of Use of British Library Reading Rooms'; The Salvation Army for its 2013 Christmas card; The Conservative Party for its 2010 general election campaign flyer; West Lodge Rural Centre for the 'Fun on the Farm' advertisement; and Karen Griggs for the 'Karen's Blinds' advertisement;

While every effort has been made to contact copyright holders, we would be pleased to hear of any that have been omitted.

Chapter 1

Introduction

> The mind is inherently embodied
> Thought is mostly unconscious
> Abstract concepts are largely metaphorical
>
> (Lakoff and Johnson 1999: 3)

This is a not a conventional book about grammar and grammar teaching. It is not a textbook, and does not offer lists of grammatical terms together with exercises and 'answers'. It is not a book that promises success in examinations by sharing hints and tips about what examination boards require. It isn't driven by a rigid assessment/objective-led pedagogy; in fact, there isn't an 'AO' in sight. And, while it acknowledges past debates about the value and status of teaching grammar, it refuses to be side-tracked into covering old ground for the sake of merely offering another academic and ideological position.

Instead, this is a book for teachers of English Language (although I would hope that teachers of English Literature would find it useful as well) that draws on recent developments in cognitive linguistics and cognitive science, academic fields that for good reasons have remained largely outside most teachers' knowledge, expertise and application. In doing so, I hope to show that these disciplines can offer teachers and researchers new ways of thinking about learning and teaching, and new ways of developing students' abilities to explore aspects of grammar, structure and meaning in purposeful and learner-centred ways. Needless to say, this is a book that also promotes the importance of language work in the English curriculum, and the importance of students being given opportunities to explore the structural, sociological and psychological dimensions of their own and others' language use. A further argument in this book is that linguistics as an academic discipline can play a critical role in developing both teachers' subject and pedagogical knowledge, and encourage them to think about their own classroom practice in new and insightful ways.

Traditionally in English schools, grammar teaching has been dominated by either formalist approaches (exploring in-built structures, rules and idealised examples of language), or by functional ones (focusing more on the wider contexts of language, the relationships between communicators and the purposes of speaking or writing). These have brought their own theoretical and, at times, political agendas with them: formal approaches tend to concentrate on language as a system of rules, and notions of correctness and standards; functional approaches have emphasised the importance of language as a social event, and associated notions of appropriateness and diversity. In most cases, each approach has largely ignored the concerns of the other; in the few cases where they have been brought together, it has been without any real coherence.

My aim in this book is to steer the debate in a different direction by exploring what some elementary principles from cognitive linguistics might have to offer the teacher in supporting teaching about grammar and meaning at post-16. As I demonstrate throughout this book, the central premise of this kind of *applied cognitive linguistic* approach is that the conceptual basis of language (including aspects of lexis, semantics and grammar) originates from experience that is rooted in physical movement and physical imagery. Consequently, the way we think, conceptualise and use language is based on our existence as physical beings, and the affordances and constraints our human-specific bodies give us in terms of viewing and making sense of the physical and abstract world. This is known as the principle of *embodied cognition*.

The influence our physical environment and experiences have on the shaping of more complex and abstract understanding can be traced back to very early infancy. Numerous studies have demonstrated that babies and very young children use and understand movement in a variety of ways and functions, drawing a sense of meaning through the various interactions they have in their immediate physical environments with objects and with their parents, and caregivers, and other children. Very young children are able to understand the notion of causality through their own manipulation of objects in their immediate space. For example, a child manipulating toys such as building blocks soon understands the concept of force as one block hits another, and subsequently reconfigures this into a conceptual model of energy transfer. In Figure 1.1 a young child pushes the blocks against each other, which results in various kinds of force as blocks move and topple over. In this instance, the child becomes aware of the causes and effects of the physical force inherent in her actions.

These kinds of primitive gestures and movements – another example would be a very young child pushing away from or moving towards an adult for attention – are more than just involuntary reactions, they are meaningful embodiments of experience and meaning, and form the basis for other, later more developed modes of expression, including language. As I explain throughout this book, this is an important and powerful idea and positions language as integrated within a broader notion of cognitive and social development, rejecting the idea that language exists in isolation from other cognitive faculties. Instead, we can view language as having a fundamental experiential basis in its forms and structures. For example, the notion of force is both an important conceptual aspect of modal forms, which denote certain attitudes or stances that a speaker holds towards an event or situation. Strong modal expressions like 'You must' contain an inherent psychological force that is analogous to a physical pressure being applied, while a weaker form such as 'You might' can be understood using the same physical terms. As I explain in Chapters 5 and 6, the notions of force and energy transfer also underpin the grammatical concept of clause transitivity (one entity doing

Figure 1.1 Building blocks and the transfer of energy

something to another entity). A cognitive approach to linguistics therefore proposes that language can be viewed as more than simply a series of arbitrary signs, and instead as inherently iconic, since an interpretative relationship exists between grammatical form and semantic content. These principles form my basis for thinking about how teachers might use this knowledge to support learners in the classroom.

Language and grammar

Arguments about the value of teaching grammar in schools and beyond have remained largely unchanged over the last 100 years. As I explain in Chapters 2 and 3, these have largely focused on two primary concerns. First, the value of dedicating valuable curriculum space to the study of something that research has shown to have little measurable impact on student competences and skills. In some schools, and for some teachers, this meant that grammar ended up being omitted entirely from classrooms. Second, the emphasis from some quarters on standards, correctness and a thinly disguised notion of linguistic policing has inevitably led to very narrow notions of what language study could look like in the classroom. This deficit view of grammar continues to have a strong hold in contemporary politics and educational policymaking, as recent changes to the English National Curriculum and Key Stage 2 testing arrangements have demonstrated. The following extract from a blog by Harry Mount published on *The Telegraph* website gives a flavour of this kind of attitude.

> Without grammar you are back in the Stone Age, reduced to making the simplest of statements; or, by trying to make more complicated ones and not being able to do it, you write nonsense. Grammar doesn't exclude; not knowing grammar does. Without good grammar, you don't have full access to one of the great joys of happening to be born in this country – being able to read and write English.
>
> (Mount 2013)

Mount's comments present a right-wing view of grammar teaching. They explicitly emphasise the notion of a correct way of speaking, and implicitly downplay non-standard forms and varieties of English. They are typical of a *prescriptive* approach to language, emphasising rules and the importance of adhering to them. By contrast, a *descriptive* approach finds value in looking at varieties of use in all forms, and linking these to specific contexts, the motivations of different writers, readers, speakers and listeners and their purposes for wanting to communicate. As I will show in Chapters 2 and 3, these competing and polarised views remain at the centre of debates both for and against the explicit teaching of language in schools.

These positions have been translated into pedagogical viewpoints that have underpinned attitudes towards grammar and language work for many years. Nearly fifty years ago, Michael Halliday drew a distinction between what he called three primary aims of grammar teaching: *productive*, *descriptive* and *prescriptive* (Halliday 1967: 83).

A productive aim focuses on the development of students' functional skills related to speaking, reading and writing. A descriptive aim is more content-driven, building students' knowledge about the language levels of discourse, semantics, syntax, lexis, morphology and graphology in ways that allow them to describe different kinds of language use accurately and systematically, with due attention to the contexts in which communication takes place. The tension between the two aims in current practice is most clearly seen in the staggering difference in focus between GCSE English Language (largely productive aims) and A level English Language (largely descriptive aims). A third aim of prescriptivism, deeply entrenched in the values of writers like Harry Mount, has moved in and out of school culture with various changes of government, policy and wider societal values. As Halliday himself remarks, it exists as

> linguistic table-manners...unlike [productive teaching]...[it] adds nothing to the pupil's linguistic abilities; it makes his performance more socially acceptable.
>
> (Halliday 1967: 83)

My aim in this book is a descriptive one, and the language ideas and concepts I examine are designed to equip students with a set of analytical resources with which they can approach, explore and discuss texts and their contexts confidently. However, I also argue that knowledge about linguistics is as valuable a tool for the teacher as it is the student. As I demonstrate throughout the book, and as numerous research studies and reports have demonstrated, one of the biggest hurdles to effective language teaching has been the lack of confidence teachers from largely literature backgrounds have had in their own subject knowledge. These colleagues are often given scant professional development opportunities both in pre-service and in-service training, and yet over time have been expected to both embrace and embed successive language and grammar initiatives. These demands have often clashed with their own identities as English teachers, which have been largely shaped by the nature of their undergraduate degrees and their initial teacher training (see Poulson *et al.* 1996).

However, the recent work by researchers at the University of Exeter on the link between contextualised grammar teaching and an improvement in students' writing, the introduction of grammar, spelling and punctuation tests at Key Stage 2, the added weighting attached to technical accuracy on GCSE papers and the continued growth of A level English Language as a viable alternative to English Literature for post-16 students all mean that it is as important as it has ever been to debate and explore the very best pedagogical models for teaching language and grammar. As Hancock and Kolln have recently argued:

> knowing about language can empower us in many ways. It can help us resist standards as well as follow them. It helps make the power and effectiveness of non-standard dialects incontrovertible fact, not just a political assertion. It can help guide us in thoughtfully nuanced expression, in recognizing the inherent connection between formal choice and rhetorical effect. The question should be about which grammar, not about when or if
>
> (Hancock and Kolln 2010: 36)

In this book, I argue that one of the ways we might do this is to look towards recent advances in linguistics and the learning sciences for ways that might empower teachers and inform their classroom practice. I firmly believe that these disciplines have the potential to offer more insightful and user-friendly ways of studying language than formalist and functional linguistic models.

Organisation of the book

This book consists of seven chapters. Following this introduction, in Chapter 2, I provide an overview of grammar and language teaching in English schools. Surveying the twentieth and the early-twenty-first centuries from the publication of the 1921 Newbolt Report to current work on GCSE and A level reform, I explore the debates surrounding grammar teaching, and the initiatives and insights from linguistics that have been filtered down to teachers in schools. I consider the relationship between the demands of the classroom and teacher subject and pedagogical knowledge, and

examine the problems associated with a pedagogy that has often attached more importance to the acquisition and use of terminology than conceptual understanding. In this
chapter I also argue that debates about language study have been dominated by political and ideological stances rather than pedagogical ones, and suggest that advances in
cognitive linguistics present an opportunity to illuminate teacher and student knowledge about how language operates.

In Chapter 3, I develop these ideas by debating the characteristics of different
models of grammar, and introducing some basic principles from cognitive linguistics to
the reader. First, I summarise the models of grammar that have formed the basis of policymaking and teaching in English schools. I show how structural and generative
models of grammar offered little to suggest that they could be adequate replacements
for a traditional latinate school grammar that had been the dominant model for the first
part of the twentieth century. By contrast, I draw on my discussion in Chapter 1 to
explain how an emerging interest in a functional linguistics in UK higher education, led
by Michael Halliday at University College London in the 1960s, filtered down into
schools and has remained, in spirit at least, as the foundation for much language work
that goes on in schools. However, the majority of this chapter is spent beginning to
explore some cognitive linguistic principles. Here, I show how cognitive linguistics
views language development as integrated into a child's general physical and intellec-
tual development, explain the inherently physical basis of conceptualisation, meaning
and, therefore grammar and exemplify the relationship between word forms and the
stores of knowledge that we have from our experience of interaction in the world.

In Chapter 4, I build on these basic principles in more detail. First, I examine how
human thought is rooted in our interaction in the physical environments in which we
live and function, and how we draw on concrete analogies to help us understand more
abstract ideas. I then draw on a number of research reports and studies from psychology and education that have shown how students may use gesture to support their
learning by making their implicit knowledge and understanding more explicit. I consequently examine some of the ways in which gesture might be useful in teaching
language and grammar in the classroom. Towards the end of the chapter, I provide
details of two case studies from the US and France, where educators have used cognitive linguistic principles to inform their pedagogical practices. These form the basis for
my own teaching model that I outline in the next two chapters.

Chapters 5 and 6 operate as a pair, providing a background set of frameworks,
concepts and terms, and a practical set of texts and activities for teachers to use. In
Chapter 5, I outline some suitable areas of study from a cognitive linguistic perspective,
in each case describing its theoretical concerns and its place within the cognitive model
of language study. I then provide an example analysis of a short text to exemplify the
model/approach and to demonstrate its explanatory and pedagogical potential. Since
this chapter informs the following one, I hope that Chapter 5 will prove useful as a
reference point for teachers. In Chapter 6, I provide detailed teaching activities using
literary and non-literary texts in a number of genres. Included for each activity are
photographs of students undertaking some of the activities and plenty of suggestions

for further work. Since the primary audience of this book is those teachers working with post-16 students at sixth form and undergraduate level, the texts I use have been selected with the ages of these students in mind. However, I have designed the activities so that they could be adapted to any year group, and differentiated to provide greater support or challenge as is appropriate. Of course I also hope teachers will find other texts in addition to the ones I've suggested that work equally as well for the students in their classes.

Finally, in Chapter 7, I review the central arguments of the book in the form of 'an embodied learning manifesto for teaching language and grammar'. Since this book is designed as an introduction to a different way of thinking about teaching, I also offer some further questions for practitioners to reflect on.

At the end of each of Chapters 1 to 5, there are suggestions for further reading that I hope teachers and researchers will find useful. My choices are necessarily selective but I feel represent books, chapters and articles that will help those wanting to continue their exploration of the matters and ideas that I have raised. I hope that these will lead to readers branching out into further exciting avenues based on their interests and preferences.

I would like to end this chapter by briefly addressing two key concerns that are central to my discussion in the remainder of this book. First, throughout the book I work with a very broad definition of grammar that necessarily goes beyond the strict linguistic domains of syntax and morphology, and at times includes aspects of meaning (semantics) and structures beyond the clause (discourse). My reasons for this are theoretical since as I explain throughout this book cognitive linguistics treats form and meaning as interrelated. In addition, cognitive linguistics often *scales up* concepts from one language level to another, for example, by demonstrating that a model has analytical potential at a lexical level, can also offer much to an analysis at the level of discourse. A good example of this can be seen in my discussion of the figure–ground phenomenon in Chapters 5 and 6. My reasons are also practical since I am interested in language study in its broadest sense and therefore want – and indeed need – to have as inclusive a set of working parameters as is possible. Since in much popular and political discourse, 'grammar' and other levels of language are often used interchangeably, I hope readers will forgive me for stretching the definition. Where possible, I do refer to 'structure' and 'meaning' separately (not least in the title of this book), but I appreciate that there are occasions where I conflate the two in using the one term.

Second, although throughout this book I insist on a pedagogy that is concept rather than terminology led, I do want to emphasise the importance of students acquiring an accurate and appropriate metalanguage with which they can explain their ideas. At various points in Chapters 5 and 6, I argue that the teacher herself must decide when to introduce terminology and how much of it is appropriate and useful for students to know. I believe that an over-reliance on the importance of terminology at the front-end of teaching has often promoted substantial barriers to learning about language for students and teachers. In these instances, terms are often 'learnt' with little understanding of the concepts they define, and in the worst cases, they become as Halliday has argued 'an alternative to clear thinking instead of an aid to it' (Halliday 1967: 87). However, I would like to stress that there is an equal danger in a teaching approach that is devoid of any attempt to encourage students to carefully and systematically use a shared metalanguage. In this instance, such teaching can simply encourage vague impressionistic comments and does little to support students long term. Throughout this book, I therefore advocate a balanced teaching approach that is concept-led but acknowledges the importance of acquiring the terminology associated with descriptive linguistics in the same way that it is with any other subject or discipline.

I'd like to end this chapter by re-enforcing my belief in the value of learning about the structures and functions of language, and my belief that such learning should be available to all within the English curriculum as a way of exploring the meanings that are shaped by people using language to communicate in various forms, to various audiences and for various purposes. I believe that descriptive linguistics can provide this kind of learning experience for all students by offering a firm grounding and 'toolkit' for them to work with precision and independence. For me, descriptive linguistics is the great leveller, providing the student of any age and ability the analytical resources with which she can make meaningful and insightful comments about her own and others' language use. This is a principle that ought to be dear to every teacher.

Further reading

Halliday (1967) is one of many articles and papers on educational linguistics by Michael Halliday that teachers might be interested in reading. The best available collection of these is Halliday (2007). Shulman (1986) explores how teachers acquire and develop various kinds of knowledge about both the content of their subject area and the best ways to teach it. Carter (1982) provides a convincing argument for the importance of linguistics to teachers. Locke (2010) is essential reading for anyone interested in the debates raised in this book and contains a range of theoretical, ideological and international perspectives. Anyone wanting to read how descriptive linguistic work can be enabling for students of all ages should read Ruth French's fascinating chapter (French 2010).

Chapter 2

Teaching grammar and language
An overview

Grammar and language teaching in English schools

In this chapter I provide an overview of relevant debates and issues in the teaching of grammar in the UK throughout the twentieth century and into the twenty-first. As the nineteenth century drew to a close, a number of debates that would shape the future of English as a subject were well under way. As Mathieson (1975) explains, students in elite private schools were thought not to need any formal education in the study of language and literature since it was presumed that they would acquire all the necessary cultural capital from their privileged lives. Instead, curricula for the elite were based on classical languages and literature, which it was believed would allow access to the admired cultural heritage of Rome and Greece and to the subsequent wisdom this would afford. By contrast, the study of English was seen as unattractive and was associated 'with working-class education, industrialism and manual labour' (Mathieson 1975: 22). As Poulson (1998) argues, while the Forster Education Act of 1870 had highlighted the importance of a universal set of functional skills and subsequently installed provision for children of lower classes to receive a basic education in literacy and numeracy, there was concern that their spiritual and moral education was being ignored. As an alternative to classical literature, the study of English culture and especially English literature quickly became seen as having the potential to hold a 'civilising and humanising influence for the middle and working classes, just as Classics did for the upper classes' (Poulson 1998: 20). This philosophy had previously been articulated by the Victorian inspector of schools and poet Matthew Arnold (Arnold 1932) who saw high-quality literature as a stabilising force with a clear social purpose in the face of rapid industrialisation, and the growth of the mass media and populist forms of writing.

The Newbolt report, published in 1921, addressed these concerns in a comprehensive discussion of all aspects and phases of English teaching from primary schools to universities to teacher training establishments. At its heart, the report emphasises social unity and the establishing of a 'common culture' drawn together through both the study of great English literature and an adherence to 'correct' ways of speaking and writing. Just as Arnold had been concerned about industrialisation and its potential to fragment society, the Newbolt report sought to address questions and factors that had been raised about the need to re-establish a unified English identity in the aftermath of the First World War. Focusing on highlighting the importance of a sense of nationhood and the improvement of social conditions for all, the report drew attention to the right of all to education. This was fuelled partly because of comparisons with other countries that had been made during the war, for example, the lack of education of English soldiers compared with their German counterparts (Poulson 1998: 24), and in the context of the advent of revolution and communism in Russia.

The rise of literature as the dominant paradigm of the English classroom can be traced through the report. Much of its content and argument focus on literature's humanising effect, and its central message is unambiguous. The committee's rejection of the appropriate nature of a classical education was based on the philosophy that children should have experiences of reading the great works of their own country as a way of securing a national identity and limiting the potential for further social division. At the heart of the report is an appeal to establishing a shared English identity and a subsequent legacy for future generations through the study of great literary works. It is littered with politicised rhetoric such as 'books are instruments through which we hear the voices of those who have known better lives than ours' (1921: 17), and argues throughout that literature teaching involves introducing students to a 'greater intellect' and 'contact with great minds' (1921: 15), whereby literature itself is 'a record of human experience' (1921: 11), which 'tell[s] us what all men are like in all countries in all times' (1921: 205). By contrast, however, the message about the value and role of knowledge about language is less clear, with many contradictory messages largely centred round the notions of judgement and correctness. The report had highlighted that having a shared language and a standardised and common way of speaking, like reading great literature, would play a part in ending social divisions. Behind this argument of course sits the ideology of attaching privilege to certain discourses and modes of speaking, demonstrated for example in the following extract.

> It is certain that if a child is not learning good English, he is learning bad English, and probably bad habits of thought; and some of the mischief done may never afterwards be undone.
>
> (Board of Education 1921: 10)

Although Standard English is identified as the model on which teachers and their students should develop 'correct pronunciation' and 'clearness and correction both in oral expression and in writing' (1921: 19), the report also criticises traditional grammar teaching in the form of rote learning, the application of latinate rules to English and an emphasis on mechanical drill-like exercises. In a section entitled 'The Problem of Grammar', the report quotes an additional study that argues that such teaching had neither improved accuracy nor supported development, and – perhaps most interestingly – had taken up time that could have been spent on the study of literature. Ironically, instead of solving 'the problem of grammar', this section of the report foregrounds several of the big debates about the value of language and grammar teaching in schools that followed throughout the remainder of the century. First, there is a lack of clarity regarding what 'grammar' means. In dismissing the usefulness of formal grammatical instruction, the report makes the case for the teaching of a 'grammar of function not form' (1921: 291) to be taught in schools, but then proceeds to define this functional grammar as a 'pure grammar [which] deals with laws which are of universal application' (1921: 291). This meaning is not consistent with what we would now consider to be a functional approach to grammar and meaning but seems to be promoting a standardised and rule-based system of communication: the 'scientific description of the facts of language' (1921: 292). Tellingly, the report also warns against teaching 'English grammar' (i.e. language as it is used and spoken) since this 'when entered upon in the classroom, [is] a territory full of pitfalls' (292).

There are two important points that are worth emphasising here. First, despite some sensible enquiry, the Newbolt report offers no consistent vision for grammar and language teaching in schools. Moreover, the term 'functional' is used in this instance to mean *instructive* rather than pointing towards a broadly descriptive or analytical model of language study. It is used in a similar way in an article by an American researcher Louis Rapeer (1913), who promotes 'drills in correct speech, and "never-failing watch and care" over the ordinary language of the classroom and playground' (1913: 132) as the basis for a coherent language pedagogy. In this way, learning about language is viewed as a utilitarian enterprise to produce desired and measurable outcomes in speech and writing. Second, the Newbolt report continued to support the rise of literature as an integral part of the English curriculum. However, with no clear guidelines or direction for grammar and language teaching its role was reduced to secondary status. In contrast, the Newbolt report's emphasis on the centrality of literature is striking. For example, in one of a number of sections recommending proposals for the teacher-training sector, the report makes it clear that teachers are to blame for 'confused and slovenly English', and suggests that in order to avoid such professional malpractice, trainers should ensure that trainee teachers have a solid grounding in literature reading and teaching, for 'the teacher should himself be in touch with such minds and such experiences [as are shown in great literary works]' (1921: 24). In one of a series of powerful rhetorical flourishes, the value of language itself as an object of study within this pedagogical model is downplayed to the point where the report stresses that when teaching and reading literature, 'the voyage of the mind should be broken as little as possible by the examination of obstacles and the analysis of the element in which the explorer is floating' (Board of Education 1921: 11).

The rising status of literature continued throughout the first half of the twentieth century. One of the members of the Newbolt committee, the Cambridge academic Sir Arthur Quiller-Couch, had previously published a series of lectures called *On the Art of Reading*, which built on the work that had been carried out at the University of Cambridge to establish English literature as a genuine discipline worthy of serious academic study. To promote this new discipline, and to ensure its longevity, Quiller-Couch continued to put forward the views of the Newbolt report by emphasising the importance of literature in teacher-training programmes and school curricula (Mathieson 1975). Later, an early literature graduate from Cambridge, F. R. Leavis expanded this philosophy into the full-blown positioning of literature as a way of developing moral and spiritual development in the face of a world that he thought was becoming increasingly filled with ephemera. The influence of the *leavisite* philosophy can be seen in a whole generation of academics in universities and teachers of English in secondary schools who shared the view of literature teaching as a civilising phenomenon, and gave primacy to reading practices that drew on the inherent power of the canonical and supremely powerful literary work to move the individual reader (Eaglestone 2002: 15).

The journey that literature took to become a valid academic discipline both at university and then in schools was not one that was available to language. As Hudson and Walmsley (2005) point out, there was no real rigorous scholarship in grammar in English universities in the twentieth century to match those who were passionately involved in developing literature as a discipline. Consequently, there was little linguistics could do as an academic and university discipline to influence what was happening in primary and secondary English classrooms. In those school classrooms, the reality was that during the first half of the twentieth century, very little actually changed in terms of how grammar and knowledge about language were taught.

The method of grammar teaching in the first part of the twentieth century is best exemplified in a series of textbooks by Ronald Ridout called *English Today*. These emphasised a 'bottom up' model of language teaching focusing on decontextualised smaller language units such as word classes, phrases and clauses, where students' work was concentrated on drills and exercises designed to improve their competence in reading and writing. The instructional aspect to this model was emphasised in Ridout's own introduction where he indicated that the primary purpose of his programme was to 'provide secondary school pupils with a complete training in the uses of their mother tongue' (Ridout 1947: 3).

A quick look at some examples from *English Today* provides a flavour of its pedagogical orientation.

> Each pair of sentences below shows an italicised word used as both an adjective and as another part of speech (verb or noun). Say what part of speech each italicised word is.
>
> 1. Tommy made himself ill eating too much *sweet* cake.
> 2. Unfortunately, Pamela tried to talk with a *sweet* in her mouth.
> 3. Can you peel an *orange* without making your fingers sticky?
> 4. *Orange* dresses rarely suit pale complexions.
>
> (Ridout 1947: 93)

What typifies this kind of exercise and approach is an insistence on the identification of formal features and the memorising of metalanguage, and the absence of any meaningful work to support students' conceptual understanding. Similar to those given above, language examples tended to be either invented, and consequently unlike those utterances spoken and read by the majority of students, or else from written nineteenth century literary texts. Carter (1990) succinctly and simply sums up this approach as 'old style grammar'.

> The exercises are furthermore constructed on a deficiency pedagogy. Pupils lack the necessary knowledge and the gaps should therefore be filled. It is of course, no accident that gap-filling is one of the main teaching and testing devices associated with such exercises with the teachers fulfilling the role of a kind of linguistic dentist, polishing here and there, straightening out, removing decay, filling gaps and occasionally undertaking a necessary extraction. The deficiency view here is that pupils lack the right language and that such deficiencies or gaps have to be made good
>
> (Carter 1990: 105–6)

In time, this 'name the parts and follow the rules' pedagogy came to be criticised by a number of research reports that explored the link between grammar teaching and competence in a student's writing, and consequently the justification for teaching grammar *per se* (see Macauley 1947, Cawley 1958 and Harris 1962). That no link could be found should hardly come as a surprise. However, as Walmsley (1984) demonstrates in reviewing what were influential condemnations of grammar teaching, the reports highlight more the inadequacies of the pedagogies that were being judged rather than make definitive judgements on the value of knowledge about language and grammar. Walmsley stresses that these reports also took little account of important variables and factors that could have influenced the reliability of results, such as the quality of teaching materials and the competence, knowledge and effectiveness of the teachers.

In the second half of the century, the climate began to change. The publication of Randolph Quirk's *The Use of English* (1962) provided the platform for value to be attached to more descriptive and enquiry-led language work, and to the development of a critical methodology for exploring language use in a range of genres and contexts (Keith 1990). In addition, there was a renewed interest in language development from psychological and sociological perspectives with their emphasis on the importance of interaction, talk and dialogue in children's linguistic achievements, and a subsequent interest in these being explored in the classroom. The influential Newsom report (Ministry of Education 1963) had identified the importance of confidence and competence in language use through the promoting and explicit discussion of talk in a variety of contexts and situations as a way of ensuring social and personal growth and improvements in educational outcomes for pupils of 'average and less than average ability' (1963: v; 19).

The interest in language as a social tool came into the classroom in the form of the government-funded *Schools Council Programme in Linguistics and English Teaching* that ran from 1964 to 1971. This was led and inspired by the work of Michael Halliday's functional approach to linguistics, and produced a range of teaching models and materials for both primary and secondary schools. In the foreword to a substantial secondary programme, *Language in Use*, Halliday had stressed the importance in education for a language awareness programme that allowed all students the opportunity to explore their own use of language in stimulating, enabling and challenging ways, and to 'realise fully the breadth and depth of its possibilities' (Doughty *et al.* 1971: 4). The *Language in Use* materials themselves provided 110 units each containing three to four lessons and divided into three broad areas of study: the nature and function of language; its place in the lives of individuals; and its role in making human society possible (Doughty *et al.* 1971: 7).

The programme sought to satisfy both the descriptive and productive aims of language teaching that Halliday had advocated for schooling (Halliday 1967), which were discussed in the introduction to this book. Students were encouraged to explore language within the boundaries of their own experience as a way of engaging with and explaining the process of meaning making. Despite its welcome focus on investigative work and the value of starting from students' own knowledge of language within their own lives, some of the activities themselves proved practically difficult for teachers and students to undertake, since they required methods of collecting data and working outside of the classroom that were alien to them (Keith 1990: 85). However, *Language in Use* influenced a new generation of textbooks in the seventies that promoted a similar spirit of enquiry-led teaching and learning centred round investigation and descriptive analysis rather than mechanical exercises and the labelling of parts of speech (Keith 1990). It demonstrated what was possible and what might be interesting for students to explore.

The Bullock committee, which had been commissioned in 1972 to report on both English teaching and teacher training, expressed the concern in its report *A Language for Life* (DES 1975) that much grammar teaching that occurred in schools was still either of the drill-based type similar to those exercises in Ridout's *English Today*, or simply was not taking place at all. Furthermore, schools and teachers were generally unaware of what exactly constituted best practice in language and grammar teaching, and so simply covered nothing. The Bullock report broke new ground in suggesting that while a return to prescriptive and drill-based grammar teaching should be avoided, all students should have access to a coherent programme of integrated and contextualised language study. Among other things, the report also recommended that every school have a policy for language across the curriculum, improved resources and pedagogies for language teaching and that language in education became an established course on all teacher-training programmes regardless of phase. In the case of the latter, although the recommendation was that this should be equivalent to 100 hours of study, the reality was that this training and its impact on teachers' practice varied from institution to institution (Poulson 1998).

The next twenty years heralded some significant changes in policy that began to address some of the Bullock report recommendations in more substantial ways. Two reports, *English from 5–16* (DES 1984) and *English from 5–16 – The Responses to Curriculum Matters* (DES 1986) put the matter of knowledge about language firmly in the minds of both the government and educators. This resulted in the Kingman Committee – chaired by a mathematician and academic from the University of Bristol

– being set up specifically to consider a theoretical pedagogical model of the English language and ways in which this might be taught to students. Foreshadowing the national curriculum, the committee was also charged with the brief of providing explicit detail about what students should be taught and be expected to know at the ages of seven, eleven and sixteen (DES 1988).

The Kingman model of language is essentially a Hallidayan one, drawing on the notion of language as a social semiotic, and reconfiguring functional linguistics into an enquiring and enabling model of language pedagogy suitable for the school classroom. It comprised four elements (see Table 2.1) that distinguished between the forms of language, the context of communication and comprehension, language acquisition and development and historical and geographical varieties of language. These formed the basis for the kinds of learning activities and knowledge that would be suitable for schools.

Dean (2003) argues that *The Teaching of English Language*, the report that discussed and disseminated the work of the Kingman committee, marked a defining moment in the discussion about teaching language and grammar since it drew clear distinctions between the processes and relative merits of descriptive and prescriptive attitudes to language. He also argues that, importantly, it rejected both the traditional grammar of the past and the belief that language study had little value in the classroom and that linguistics had nothing to offer education. Together with Halliday's pioneering work, this report had as much influence in the promotion of language work as a genuine school subject as did the move towards a national curriculum, and with it the growing debate about grammar and correctness that had resurfaced. The Cox Report, *English 5–16* (DESWO 1989), took this further with its aim to establish curricular and assessment content for the imminent national curriculum, raising questions about the need for an explicit kind of language teaching in the context of the Conservative government's pressing desire to establish that document and its ensuing framework for teachers.

All of this led naturally to the commissioning of the Language in the National Curriculum (LINC) project in 1989, designed to produce teaching materials and

Table 2.1 The Kingman Model (from DES 1988)

Part	Content
1. The forms of the English language	Elements of mode (speech and writing); aspects of lexis and semantics, syntax, discourse structure
2. Communication and comprehension	A model of communication that is informed by context, genre and the social, cultural and cognitive aspects of interaction
3. Acquisition and development	Child language acquisition, and the development of language and literacy skills through education and interaction with others
4. Historical and geographical variation	How languages change over time and vary according to region

resources following the Kingman and Cox Reports with their emphases on the need for a standardised model of language teaching and a national training programme for teachers. Focusing largely on the third part of the Kingman model and equally inspired by Halliday's functional linguistics, the programme, led by Ronald Carter of the University of Nottingham and supported by 150 other education professionals over a two-year period of writing, proposed a new model of language for education that was largely functional and discourse based. While still attaching significance to aspects of linguistic form, the LINC model emphasised that language was a system of choice governed by ideological and other contextual influences, and was open to explicit and critical analysis. The dissemination of teaching materials to schools was based on a cascade system whereby expert nominated advisers from a local education authority (LEA) would train heads of English, who in turn would train their colleagues (the model was repeated in the national strategies training from 2000 onwards). In many ways, the LINC project was a curious phenomenon. Although innovative and progressive in terms of its applied linguistic pedagogy and the importance it attached to students and teachers being able to describe language consciously in an explicit and common metalanguage, it was funded by a Conservative government with a very different view of what and how students should be taught in schools. When government ministers realised that this functional and social model of language did not mirror their own views that teaching should focus on the grammar of sentences and enable students to become better users of Standard English, the programme was stopped. Having previously promised to provide a copy of the LINC training materials to every secondary school in England and Wales, the government now refused not only to publish the materials but also to allow them to be taken on and published by any third party. The official view was that the materials were considered as suitable for developing teachers' own knowledge and understanding of language, but wholly inappropriate for use in the classroom with students. There is a subtle yet crucial distinction here that becomes apparent in the words of Tim Eggar, an education minister who claimed that the central concern of the government – and presumably teachers – 'must be the business of teaching children how to use their language *correctly*' (Eggar 1991, added emphasis). The LINC programme and materials were savaged in a series of attacks by the right-wing press on what they saw as the deeply subversive pedagogy it encouraged. One such report, with a combination of breathtaking prejudice and crude ignorance, bemoaned the fact that the project would still be available to

> teacher training institutions where its voodoo theories about the nature of language [that] will appeal to the impressionable mind of the young woman with low A-levels in 'soft subjects' who, statistically speaking, is the typical student in these establishments. And there is the rub. In another 10 years, the same student will contribute to another LINK (sic) report saying much the same thing in even more desolate language.
>
> (Walden 1991)

Pedagogical and political differences aside, LINC's other problem was operational. The length of the materials and the required knowledge of the theoretical frameworks that teachers would need meant that crucial pedagogical concepts were not always received as intended, and both the collaborative writing and heavy editing that characterised the work meant that at times certain key messages were not always clear (Sweetman 1991). In addition, the cascade model itself proved problematic, with some schools claiming that the training they received was either poor or non-existent (Poulson 1998: 75). However, the legacy of the LINC materials lives on, particularly in A level English Language specifications such as those run by the AQA examination board, which emphasise the importance of studying contexts, genre, varieties of language use and speech, as well as in the recent but sadly short-lived filtering down of spoken language as a topic worthy of study at Key Stage 4. In addition, teaching materials that promote the critical exploration of language in its social contexts have continued to be produced and well received by English departments (see, for example, the recent British Telecom *All Talk* training materials for spoken language study).

The period following Kingman, Cox and LINC was dominated by prefaces to the national strategies that started in primary schools and transferred into secondary schools at the turn of the century. During this time, two publications *The Grammar Papers: Perspectives on the Teaching of Grammar in the National Curriculum* and *Not Whether but How: Teaching Grammar in English at Key Stages 3 and 4* (QCA 1998, 1999) offered interesting research-led perspectives on grammar and language teaching. The top-down and centralised pedagogies of the strategies continued to maintain this focus, but began to emphasise and promote an alternative skills-focused technical model of English, highlighting the importance for example of using complex sentences and a wider range of punctuation at the expense of one that saw language and grammar as creative and critical resources (Clark 2010).

Language work has always had to justify its place, and its validity and credibility as a part of the English curriculum has often depended not on whether the study of language *per se* is a valuable exercise but whether learning about language and grammar has been shown to have any discernible effect on writing competence. As I have previously explained, the research evidence has tended to dismiss rather than support its claims. However, recent work by Debra Myhill and her team at Exeter University (see Myhill *et al.* 2012) has found a clear causal relationship between a contextualised and explicit type of teaching that makes meaningful connections between grammar and its use in composition. The Exeter model is largely a model of enabling and exploring choice in lexical and syntactic units and patterns, and as such promotes a pedagogy that is essentially a form of 'writing as rhetoric', which acknowledges language as a system of choice from which linguistic forms can be chosen depending on the context of writing, and in particular its audience and purpose. The reconfiguration of grammar into a set of language resources from which students can make informed and deliberate choices based on aspects of genre, purpose, readership and aesthetics offers the potential for a powerful new discourse of language teaching in schools. What Myhill's work has also done is to provide a renewed opportunity to debate the pedagogic value of different kinds of grammar teaching.

The relationship between grammar, rhetoric and writing is an interesting one, and one that already has a significant profile in higher education, where *stylistics* (see, for example, Simpson 2014) is a thriving discipline that draws on linguistic theory primarily in the service of critical response and interpretation of literary and non-literary texts. Indeed, on some higher education courses in English, there has been a clear focus on using linguistics as a way of improving writing. For example at Middlesex University in London, Dr Billy Clark's innovative and highly successful third-year undergraduate 'Writing Techniques' module offers students from a variety of backgrounds and different academic pathways the opportunity to use linguistic knowledge explicitly to support their own writing in a variety of forms.

In establishing a link between grammar teaching and improved outcomes in writing, the Exeter team's work both revisits old battlegrounds and shapes the next chapter of the grammar debate. One of the most important research findings was that both teacher experience and subject knowledge were significant influential factors in determining whether students benefited from any explicit work on grammar and language. Although I return to these points later in this chapter, it is worth some brief comment now. The research highlighted the fact that very experienced and very inexperienced teachers were found to use the intervention materials that the researchers had put together less successfully. Equally, teachers with weaker subject knowledge had limited success, either relaying incorrect terminology and definitions to their students or else promoting the use of generalised and superficial comments about perceived content and its effect (e.g. using adjectives adds 'impact'), a practice that the team called the dissemination of 'meaningless grammar' (Myhill *et al.* 2012: 159). The matter of insufficient or incomplete teacher subject knowledge is one that has been a topic of debate from the Newbolt report in 1921, and has been identified as one of the major factors in part for grand and costly projects such as LINC and the national strategies not having the impact that was originally intended for them.

A more recent set of centrally imposed changes also highlights the importance of teacher knowledge, and at the same time drags the debate about language and grammar teaching into some rather familiar territory. The Bew report (DfE 2011), formed to look at Key Stage 2 assessment and accountability, recommended that while writing composition was best assessed internally by teachers, more technical aspects such as spelling, punctuation, vocabulary and grammar 'where there are clear "right" or "wrong" answers' (2011: 14) should be externally tested. The first Year 6 students sat this test in the summer of 2013, and it would be fair to say that public, professional and academic reaction to the tests has been mixed. While there has been considerable anxiety over a seemingly regressive and retrospective 'naming and labelling of parts' pedagogy, the explicit teaching (and testing) of language has been welcomed at least cautiously by those interested in and working at the interface of linguistics and education. The subsequent changes to the curriculum to specify the kinds of knowledge that students should have and will be tested on are also interesting. The Key Stages 1 and 2 Programme of Study specify for example that by the end of Year 4, students should be introduced to terminology including 'noun phrase', 'direct speech', 'determiner', 'preposition' and 'adverbial', and should be able to use these terms when discussing aspects of their reading and their own writing (DfE 2013a). As I write, the recently published Key Stage 3 National Curriculum (DfE 2013b) includes a non-statutory glossary of grammatical terms, intended as a guide for teachers, and its range of study requires students to apply and extend their grammatical knowledge from the Key Stages 1 and 2 national curriculum programmes of study. However, the subject content for Key Stage 4 (DfE 2013c), from which awarding bodies have devised GCSE speci-fications, has very little that is focused on language, and has removed the compulsory study of spoken language. Instead it reintroduces some of the rhetoric of previous generations in its references to Standard English and notions of 'correctness'. In fact, the overall future of explicit grammatical teaching at compulsory secondary level is still unclear and we might well end up with the curious irony of primary teachers who are much better prepared and knowledgeable in aspects of grammar and language than their secondary counterparts.

The growth of A level English Language

The rapid and significant growth of A level English Language over the last thirty years has provided both a high-quality post-16 option in language study and a valuable and viable alternative to English Literature. While not being subjected to the same kinds of initiatives and controversies that have dogged language and grammar teaching in compulsory education, the history of the subject at post-16 is not completely straight-forward. The first A level English in 1951 was an A level in 'English' and largely literature orientated, and this continued to be the case for a long time. Although the Secondary Schools Examinations Council's 1964 report had recommended that an alternative 'language' paper be included as an option for A level students to take (DES 1964), and had included a draft syllabus and examination written by Randolph Quirk, who had later presented this overview for an A level Modern English Language in the first bulletin of the newly formed *National Association for the Teaching of English* (Gibbons 2013), it was nearly twenty years before anything resembling a genuine examination component actually materialised. However, the renewed interest in univer-sities in linguistics from the early 1960s onwards led to an interest in language work filtering down into schools, and initiatives and innovative programmes designed to increase awareness of language among students beginning to occur at 'grass roots' level. For example, Creek (1967) presents a comprehensive account of a language study course designed for and taught to sixth form students, which focuses on a range of linguistic content. The scope of study including the sound system of English, lexis and semantics, grammar, language and representation, language and context and language and style would feel very familiar to an A level teacher over forty years on. Indeed, in some respects, the course also feels beyond its time with the study of metaphor in non-literary 'everyday' discourse, the registers of occupational groups and the comparison of human language to animal communication systems.

In 1981, 42 students took an experimental optional paper in 'varieties of English' offered by the University of London, the first opportunity offered by an awarding body for sixth form students to sit an examination in English language (Hawkins 1984). The London version of A level English Language evolved to be a specification that was largely concerned with structures and language as a system, and more in line with linguistics as it was taught in higher education. An alternative specification, which had its origins in discussions held at the Schools Council English 16–19 Project Conference in 1978, was set up by the Joint Matriculation Board (JMB), comprising the universities of Manchester, Liverpool, Birmingham and Sheffield (Scott 1989). This was less driven by formal linguistics, was more sociologically orientated in its nature, and was influenced greatly by the kind of 'language study' work that Halliday's school programme in the 1960s and early 1970s had promoted and disseminated. Over the years, the JMB model has morphed through various examination board mergers to be most easily recognised in the AQA specifications (A and B up until 2015 and a single specification under A level reform). The growth of the subject is staggering. In 1985 the first JMB specification had 210 entries mostly from the north-west of England although some schools from other parts of the country did manage to enter small cohorts of sixth formers who took the A level as an additional subject. By 2012, AS entry for all English Language specifications nationally stood at nearly 35,000 candidates, with almost 24,000 candidates continuing to take the subject to a full A level. At the time of writing, the AQA specifications account for around 80 per cent of the A level English Language market.

Angela Goddard (personal communication) explains the popularity of the JMB version of A level English Language in the context of the changing climate of linguistics and language studies in higher education. In the 1970s, research driven by new advances and theories in sociology was influencing those working in linguistics departments, who began to develop courses that were less influenced by structural and psychological studies. In turn, interested teachers who had taken undergraduate and/or postgraduate qualifications in linguistics with significant sociolinguistic elements sought ways in which they could use their newly acquired knowledge to explore language with their classes, and offer a qualification in their schools that was a viable alternative to English Literature. This interest from teachers was fed back into higher education, where academics who were working at the interface of linguistics, language studies, sociology and education saw the value in continuing to develop and promote a new type of qualification that would naturally build on teachers' interests, follow on from lower-school study and provide skills that would allow progression both to higher education programmes and to employment.

The success of the AQA brand of English Language is in part due to the way it has carved out a strong identity for itself as an 'accessible' subject that draws on what teachers and students know about language in non-threatening ways while still being driven by the kinds of rigorous study of language and linguistics in higher education. Its growth and popularity are remarkable for a subject area that is still dominated by entrants who have academic backgrounds in English Literature.

Grammar teaching and teachers

Both the Bullock and the Kingman reports had highlighted the importance of teacher subject knowledge and confidence as factors in securing an effective programme of native language study in secondary schools. In reviewing how both the LINC project and the language components of the national curriculum were received by English teachers, Poulson *et al.* (1996) found that many departments where literature had held a central place in the curriculum and schemes of work were unprepared for a greater emphasis on language teaching, and many found the cascade model that the programme had relied on to be unsatisfactory. The authors argue that the requirement to incorporate language study also challenged teachers' professional identities, which for many were shaped by a background in the study of English literature, and did not easily accommodate the skills and content of linguistics. Other studies present similar accounts of concerns regarding subject knowledge and teacher identity. Watson (2012) draws attention to the anxiety – and in some cases antipathy – that teachers can feel towards grammar and its place in and impact on their philosophy and practice of English teaching. This anxiety about subject knowledge is likely to be one of the reasons why centrally directed initiative after initiative has never quite reached the dizzy heights for which it was intended. For example, writing about the LINC project, Colin Hughes argues that

> the critical problem with the 'new grammar' is not that it is 'wacky', or 'trendy', or even that it is complacent about standards; it is that the methods are extremely demanding of the teacher, requiring extensive knowledge of language. Moreover, they require that all teachers, not just English teachers, become conscious of the way children are using language. In truth, probably only a minority of teachers feel confident about delivering the national curriculum's language learning targets; many, it must reasonably be suspected, may not have entirely understood them.
>
> (Hughes 1991: 23)

Comparing the relative academic backgrounds of English teachers in terms of their undergraduate study offers a pretty convincing example of why this might be the case. In their survey of PGCE trainees and tutors, Blake and Shortis (2010) found that institutions attached greater value to literature undergraduate degree than ones in language, linguistics or media studies. Their research also found that the percentage of trainee teachers coming onto course with single honours qualifications in English language or linguistics was low (3 per cent and 0.8 per cent, respectively) compared with 37 per cent in English literature. Equally, there was a tendency for concern and remedial action on aspects of subject knowledge to be more keenly felt when they involved aspects of literary study rather than language.

Subject knowledge and our own confidence in that knowledge as teachers have of course always been important. The Newbolt report had drawn attention to the need to have specialist and expert teachers of English literature and elevated the status and the role of the teacher to that of evangelical missionary, certain in the belief that

literature and life are inseparable, that literature is not just a subject for academic study, but one of the chief temples of the human spirit, in which all should worship.
(Board of Education 1921: 259)

Some sixty years on, Michael Halliday asserted a similarly important role for the teacher of English language by emphasising the need for 'the professionally trained English language teacher' (1967: 81). However, since English as a subject has been compartmentalised into separate disciplines with an undue privilege afforded to the study of literature, the reality is that the majority of trainee teachers do not have the language/linguistics backgrounds from which they can be comfortable teaching. In many cases, such an inherent gap in subject knowledge is unlikely to be filled during initial teacher training. On my own university's core PGCE programme, where around 65% of trainees have no background in language/linguistics (which includes modern foreign languages and classics), traditionally only three to six hours a year have been devoted to language topics. As Bluett *et al.* (2004: 12) argue, on teacher training programmes it has historically been 'a hit and miss matter as to whether a PGCE student gains any real experience of the subject [English Language]'. The current coalition government's drive towards making *School Direct* the default model for initial teacher training means that it is possible that trainees will have even less exposure to language teaching or simply none at all. Despite the growth of A level language as a post-16 subject, we could be left with insufficiently equipped teachers to teach it. Anecdotally it seems as though more teachers are being asked to teach the subject at post-16 without being given appropriate training and support.

The question raised by Poulson *et al.* (1996) regarding how teacher subject knowledge fits into other forms and notions of knowledge and practice is worth returning to at this point. In an evaluation of the role of linguistics in primary teacher education and practice, Ellis and Briggs (2011) are critical of the kind of objectivist accumulative piece-by-piece view of teacher knowledge that is then assumed to be transmitted to pupils by means of a 'what is in our heads simply migrates into yours' approach (2011: 276). They argue that such an approach ignores the social–cultural context of learning, and aspects of knowledge construction through action and interaction in the classroom. Such a view also espouses an over-simplified conceptualisation of subject knowledge as a crude tick list of terms on a subject audit, without considering the questions of what 'subject knowledge look[s] like in practice, how might it be conceptualised, and what is its relationship to classroom teaching' (2011: 283). The authors exemplify this superficial view in discussing a case study where a group of teachers had taken on a specific pedagogy uncritically and without fully understanding the concepts behind it, and as a consequence struggled to fit the model into their practice in a meaningful and impactful way. In a similar way, Myhill (2000) provides examples of non-specialist language teachers finding it difficult to explain grammatical concepts to students, since despite having learnt the terminology, they were not confident in their understanding of the concepts behind the terms. In both of these examples, the pressure to acquire and teach *terminology* has been given greater prominence than acquiring a firm conceptual basis from which to make decisions about teaching and learning and consider how knowledge about grammar and language might fit in with other kinds of pedagogical knowledge and activity.

Conclusion

I would argue that there has been too much debate on grammar and language from ideological perspectives (notions of correctness, standards, failing teachers and students) rather than pedagogical ones, and from competing discourses from both within the subject and within the profession itself. Furthermore, the discourse of grammar has been characterised by an increasingly unhelpful emphasis on utility: grammar has either been championed as the saviour of falling standards, or been dismissed if it cannot prove to have measurable impact on skills of some kind. Indeed the value of whether linguistics in itself might be a discipline deserving of study in schools in the same way as say history or chemistry has been conveniently ignored. In response to this question, Walmsley (1984) asks why there is a need to justify teaching grammar on the basis of whether it can prove measurable outcomes, whereas this isn't the case for either literature – do we have to justify teaching Shakespeare on the grounds that reading him will improve reading or writing skills – or indeed for other subjects.

> Instead of allowing linguistics to be tied to written performance as the only admissible criterion, ought we not to demand that any child should have the right to study his or her own native **language** in all its aspects? Why should such a study need more special justification than any other subject? The argument that it cannot be shown to improve their practical written performance smacks of a depressing philistinism totally irreconcilable with a humane or liberal approach to the curriculum.
>
> (Walmsley 1984: 9 original emphasis)

In contrast to traditional models of language, cognitive linguistics proposes that language is not a separate, autonomous system but operates in line with other cognitive processes that are embedded in social activity. As I suggest in the next chapter, this makes for a plausible alternative model of thinking about language that might be applied in the classroom, since it has an accessible and understandable conceptual basis, and is rooted in recent developments from cognitive science that demonstrate how we organise information in the mind and use language as a way of expressing conceptual content. It is also consonant with other kinds of knowledge that we have as teachers about how students learn, and how we might organise the classroom and activities to support that learning.

Further reading

The Newbolt, Kingman, Cox and other reports referred to in this chapter are all accessible online (www.educationengland.org.uk). This is a comprehensive site run by Derek Gillard that contains over 320 official reports and documents pertaining to education as a well as a detailed written history of education in England from 597 to 2010 (Gillard 2011). Mathieson (1975), Poulson (1998) and Dean (2003) all provide good overviews on English curricula teaching in schools, and Eaglestone (2002) and Goddard (2012) give informative discipline-specific accounts of the identities of English Literature and English Language. Locke (2010) has a comprehensive overview of matters related to grammar teaching in the UK, US and Australia, while Halliday (1967) and Carter (1982) offer various accounts on the value and application of linguistics in schools. Elley *et al.* (1979) provide details of research and doctoral theses on grammar and writing from 1950 to 1970, and Wyse (2001) and Andrews *et al.* (2006) provide more recent summaries of research against the value of grammar teaching. By contrast, Walmsley (1984) and Tomlinson (1994) discuss flaws in a number of research methodologies and findings. The LINC Reader (ed. Carter 1990) is the best overview of the principles and content of the LINC project. Richmond (1992) and Carter (1996) discuss these principles and the pedagogies that were developed from them in the context of the government's subsequent banning of the LINC teaching resources. For those unable to get a copy of the original materials, Bain (1991) gives a good flavour of the kinds of work that were promoted. Sealey (1994) explores press coverage of the LINC project in the context of the various political stances and ideological concerns of the time. Cajkler (2004) and Wales (2009) offer interesting accounts of some of the problems in linguistic content and detail in national strategy documentation. The work and findings of Debra Myhill and her team are discussed in several outputs, see, for example, Myhill (2011), Myhill *et al.* (2012) and Myhill *et al.* (2013). Wyse *et al.* (2013) offer a critique of Myhill's work. Those looking for an introduction to stylistics should consult Simpson (2014) and Carter and Stockwell (2008) for good overviews. Clark and Owtram (2012) discuss and review aspects of the 'Writing Techniques' module at Middlesex University. Goddard and Beard (2007) and Bluett *et al.* (2004) explore key aspects of A level English Language. The education section of Dick Hudson's website www.dickhudson.com/education has a wealth of material of interest to the secondary English teacher, including statistics on entry for all A level English subjects. Creek (1967) offers a fascinating overview of a sixth form English language and linguistics programme that was taught in the 1960s. Scott (1989) dedicates a whole chapter to a comparison of the first JMB and London Board A level English Language specifications. Hawkins (1984) surveys a range of other school initiatives in the teaching of English language and linguistics in schools, and Tinkel (1988), Shuttleworth (1988) and Goddard (1993) demonstrate the type of investigative work that typified early A level specifications. Williamson and Hardman (1995), Cajkler and Hislam (2002), Borg (2003) and Watson (2012) all report on teachers' knowledge of and attitudes to grammar in the context of their own professional practice and identity.

Chapter 3

Why should teachers be interested in cognitive linguistics?

From traditional and functional to cognitive linguistics

In the last chapter, I provided an overview of language and grammar teaching in schools. In this section, I provide a description of the models of grammar that have formed the basis for policymaking and teaching in the UK. The default model in schools until the 1960s had been what might be loosely termed *traditional* or *school grammar*. This was a largely prescriptive grammar that treated English in the same way as classical languages, such as Latin and Greek, and used these as a benchmark for a type of idealised grammar. Consequently, this promoted an emphasis on notions of 'correct forms', the privileged status of Standard English and the belief that deviations from grammatical norms were deficiencies of some kind. This is the type of pedagogy evident in Ronald Ridout's *English Today* books, with their emphasis on the naming of parts and drill-like exercises focusing exclusively on largely invented examples of written language. As I demonstrated in Chapter 2, it was this kind of grammar teaching that was criticised throughout the twentieth century as being dull to teach, having little impact on students' understanding of language and no direct effect on their competence in writing. As I also explained, the pedagogies associated with this form of language study played a large role in the demise of explicit grammar and language teaching in schools, and its subsequent devaluing by the teaching profession.

Advances in linguistic theory in higher education in the middle of the twentieth century presented more scientific models of language that could offer alternative pedagogical ones. In the US, though not in the UK, *structural grammar* and *generative grammar* became established as alternatives to traditional grammar in educational discourse and practice, although it is debatable whether they had any meaningful value and impact in the classroom (Hancock and Kolln 2010).

Structural grammar as a pedagogy worked from the assumption that as language was built out of small discrete parts that formed larger patterns, these patterns or structures were worthy of study to both develop students' knowledge of the ways in which their own language operated, and to provide templates for learning other languages. While such approaches were concerned largely with formal features, they did acknowledge some limited aspects of the social and contextual dimensions of language and communication.

On the other hand, generative grammar (e.g. Chomsky 1957) took a more inwards-looking, psychological stance by arguing that language was a series of internalised rules from which an infinite number of instances of sentences and utterances could be generated. Generative grammarians were mostly concerned with how idealised rules could be explained as mental operations rather than with looking at language use in practice. In this model, the social and contextual dimensions of language were downplayed to the point that they became irrelevant, since actual examples of language in use, as varied as they were, would do little to explain deep structures and rules, or rival them as worthy of linguists' study. Another major generative principle was that language was an innate phenomenon acquired through a *universal grammar* that exists in all humans and was set to enable the language user to automatically acquire language from birth. In this model, language is viewed as a discrete phenomenon, operating under its own parameters, separated from other forms of cognitive functioning and development. The generative stance assumes that the part of the brain responsible for language functioning is separate from that responsible for governing other general facets of cognition. The consequent pedagogical principle is that language teaching is not best served by the explicit study of grammar in any form, or by looking at real examples of language use and paying attention to the social dimension of communication and meaning. Instead, whole language approaches through the exposure to worthy forms of stimulus such as great literature and opportunities for creative writing are considered enough to develop both communicative competence and meta-linguistic awareness (Hancock and Kolln 2010: 27). In these terms, generative pedagogical principles are effectively redundant ones since they downplay the importance of detailed linguistic and contextual study in the classroom.

In the UK, both the demise of research in linguistics in higher education and the lack of a genuinely pedagogical grammar can help to explain the gradual decline of grammar teaching in schools. As I explained in Chapter 2, the groundbreaking work by Michael Halliday in the 1960s offered an alternative *descriptive* rather than prescriptive view of language. This emphasised the functional and the contextual macro-aspects of text and discourse as well as the formal micro-components of lexis, morphology and syntax. Halliday's *systemic functional linguistics*, including his model of *functional grammar*, is a top-down model of communication that starts with big-picture phenomena such as the social context, the topic of communication, the relationship between writer/speaker and reader/listener and the mode of expression (writing, speech or a hybrid of the two). It emphasises the fact that language occurs in social contexts between socially motivated participants, values speech as well as writing, uses authentic texts rather than invented examples to demonstrate language in use and attaches a central importance to meaning that had previously been reserved for form. In this model, grammar is viewed as a semiotic resource for language users to make meaning rather than a set of prescriptive rules that they should follow.

This functional model of language was the basis of much of the socially orientated investigative work that followed Halliday's *Schools Council Project* that I described in Chapter 2, and underpinned the LINC pedagogy and materials. Following Halliday's move to Australia in the early 1970s, functional approaches to language emerged as dominant pedagogies there, forming the basis of both teaching about grammar and genre-based literacy programmes (see for example Rose and Martin 2012). Post-LINC, the influence of Hallidayan linguistics in the UK has been felt in the genre-based pedagogy that marked the Key Stage 3 strategy writing materials. In the US, functional approaches to language and grammar teaching can be found in holistic pedagogies such as *meaning-centred grammar* (Hancock 2005) and *rhetorical grammar* (Kolln and Gray 2012).

While the limitations of traditional or school grammar that offer a deficit view of language have been widely discussed and discredited in research outputs, it should be noted that even the most comprehensive of these, Andrews *et al.* (2006), did not examine or comment on the value and impact of functional grammar as a pedagogical tool. Indeed, although there has been no empirical evidence to support the value of functional approaches, there are a number of case studies and accounts of authentic classroom experience that have been validated by teachers and researchers (see for example Williams 1998, Burns and Knox 2005, Macken-Horarik 2009 and French 2010).

There is an obvious attraction to functional grammar's emphasis on the importance of meaning and its relation to lexical and grammatical choices, and on the centrality of context as a motivator for linguistic decision-making. Indeed, the A level specifications, primarily those offered by the AQA examination board, which have retained a functional spirit and a discourse-based approach to language and textual study, have been hugely popular with students and teachers. In a broader context, systemic functional linguistics has been promoted as being beneficial to teachers to inform their responses to and assessment of student writing as well as being an analytical tool for students. Researchers have argued that the model offers much broader and inclusive ways of thinking about learning and teaching than traditional models (see for example Macken-Horarik 2012, Berry 2013).

However, there are several limitations relating to functional grammar and linguistics as models of language for the classroom. First, they can promote the idea that there is no need to focus on grammatical form at all, and instead concentrate simply on bigger-picture details of context and discourse. This kind of approach can lead to students being skilled in articulating a great deal about the contexts in which language events take place, but unable to describe the language itself. It therefore has the potential to allow students to rely on an idiosyncratic rather than a systematic method of description. Viewed in this way and from both theoretical and pedagogical perspectives, language is understood too simplistically as a response to social circumstances, independent of any psychological basis or cognitive architecture. In this regard, a functional perspective could be conceived as limited – albeit in a different way – as a generative model of language that offers idealised forms of language without any reference to actual examples of that language in the real world. In addition, functional grammar, even at a basic level, requires a considerable amount of new theory and knowledge that most teachers will just not have. As was demonstrated with the LINC materials and the

Key Stage 3 strategy, if a theoretical tool is not user-friendly, its impact will remain limited. Finally, although a key principle of functional linguistics is its social emphasis, from a teaching perspective it can look as abstract as other models. Consequently, it doesn't offer an obviously practical way into learning and doesn't necessarily place language as part of an inter-related set of cognitive processes and functions that can be drawn on as part of pedagogical practice.

My argument in the next section of this chapter, and then throughout the remainder of this book, is that teachers could benefit from exploring the potential of a relatively new branch of linguistics as a teaching tool. Cognitive linguistics aims to recognise both the social, contextual and psychological dimensions of language, and provides different ways for teachers to think about language and how some key aspects of grammar and meaning might be taught to students. Since it is a new discipline the parameters of which are still to be fully agreed by linguists, and since my interest is primarily to explain the potential value of the discipline in an educational context, my focus will necessarily be on small and particular parts of the body of work that has been undertaken. In the next part of this chapter I present some preliminary discussion of a select number of principles that cognitive linguistics offers, and suggest a way in which these might support classroom practice. These ideas will be more fully developed and exemplified for the classroom teacher in Chapters 4, 5 and 6.

1   Language uses the same set of cognitive processes as other areas of knowledge and learning

In cognitive linguistics, language is not viewed as an autonomous entity that is acquired in a special way, as in Chomsky's generative grammar, or one that operates in distinctive and exclusive ways, but instead is understood as one of a number of inter-related cognitive functions we use to learn and make sense of our surroundings and experiences. Since language is a way of expressing our conceptualisations of events and experiences, which in themselves are always filtered through our 'species-specific neural and anatomical architecture' (Tyler 2012: 28), we construct a view of reality that is informed by our human capacities and limitations, and by our interaction with the social and physical world.

An obvious example of this inter-relatedness would be to consider the ways in which our perceptual systems organise incoming stimuli and experiences. When we open our eyes, what we 'see' is a certain type of arrangement, where some aspects of the scene are afforded attention (for example through being colourful, bright or having its parameters clearly marked) while others are relegated to the background. This is true at all times, even though the relationship in the scene is essentially a dynamic one, and we can re-configure scenes so that other entities are brought into attention and previous ones become part of the background. In cognitive psychology, this arrangement is understood as the difference between a *figure* (the entity that stands out) and the *ground* (the de-emphasised background aspects). Clearly, if we didn't have this capacity to assign prominence to certain aspects then what we would see (and indeed hear, smell or touch) would be completely disorganised. Cognitive linguists argue that we also see this principle operating in language. For example, in English we would normally speak of the scene shown in Figure 3.1 as 'the book is on the table'. Here the grammar of the clause mirrors our conceptualisation of the visually smaller entity, the book, standing out as prominent against the larger background of the table. A conventionalised pattern thus emerges in the way that the preposition 'on' is used to both express the relationship between two objects of differing sizes and to present that grammatically with the prominent entity at the beginning of the clause. A different way of expressing the same event but with 'book' and 'table' occupying the same positions in the clause, 'the table is under the book' would sound unnatural. However, the use of 'under' to represent the relationship between the two entities shown in Figure 3.2 in 'the cat is under the table' seems natural given their relative sizes, and again reflects our natural orientation to emphasise the smaller entity as a focus against a larger background, which is replicated in the grammar. An alternative way of presenting the scene such as 'the table is over the cat', feels very odd indeed, and we might not expect to find it used, unless to create some strikingly original effect, for example in a genre of writing such as surrealist poetry.

Figure 3.1 'The book is on the table'

Figure 3.2 'The cat is under the table'

2 Meaning is embodied through the interaction of our bodies in the physical world

The examples above demonstrate the ways in which language use and meaning have strong bases in our physical world. This is known as the *embodied nature of meaning*. We can consider this in more detail by thinking about the prominence we attach to sight as a way of navigating our environment, recognising people and places and undertaking tasks. Being able to see is important and meaningful to us as physical beings in order to move within our physical environment, and this meaningfulness is extended into expressions by which we conceptualise the more abstract notion of understanding, for example, as in 'I can see that now' and 'that's really clear to me'. In a similar way, human bodies are bipedal and consequently position us vertically: we stand and move for the majority of the time in an upright position. This has meaning in our everyday interaction in the world – the ways in which we travel, build houses, play sports and so on – and has a fundamental role in the ways that we organise our conceptual systems and the kinds of linguistic expressions we use to express ideas, thoughts and feelings. For example, in western cultures, 'I'm feeling low' is a common way of talking about unhappiness, and is related to our natural disposition to re-orient ourselves downwards physically when faced with such an emotion (Lakoff and Johnson 1980: 15). By contrast, phrases like 'I'm on a real high' are meaningful through their relationship to a more upright stance that often accompanies moments of elation.

A further example of this can be understood by considering general knowledge that is gained through our experience of an interaction in the world, such as the understanding that one thing can be physically contained in another, for example, in a box or a building. In Chapter 5, I explain how such basic templates for organising experience are understood as examples of mental *image schemas* that are built up from birth through our interaction with the immediate physical environment and are used as ways of understanding simple relationships. These schemas in turn provide a structure for understanding more complex conceptual content. For example, the idea of 'containment' offers a mental template for explaining a relationship between two entities where one is contained in another using 'in' at the head of a prepositional phrase in the expression 'the water is in the bucket'. It also provides knowledge of potential physical constraints and consequences that have functional significance: we understand dropping a bucket with water in will usually result in the water being spilled. Furthermore, this 'template' underpins our conceptual understanding of expressions that have similar linguistic formulations such as 'I'm in a mood' and 'I'm not in a mood anymore', where an emotion becomes conceptualised and understood as a bounded entity, which just like a container, we can move in or out of either of our own volition or directed by some external agency.

3 Words act as reference points to stores of knowledge that we use to communicate with each other

In the following exchange, speaker A is asking speaker B the directions to the bank.

> A: Can you tell me where the bank is please?
> B: Yes, it's next to the supermarket, there [points in the direction of the bank]
> A: Oh, I see yes, thank you

Cognitive linguistics proposes that words offer access points to stores of knowledge called *frames* that are vital for communication and the ways in which we can have meaningful dialogue with other people. In the exchange above, speaker A's choice of the word 'bank' is governed by the situation and purpose of communication (wanting to get to the bank) and, when used, acts a trigger to a frame of associated knowledge that speaker B holds (what a bank is, why A might want to go to the bank/the sorts of things that people do in banks and so on). This leads to a successful communicative exchange. In this instance, the speakers' joint use and understanding of the word also relies on both of them being able to access a range of *embodied encyclopaedic knowledge* that has been experienced over time such as visiting a bank, speaking to clerks there, paying in money, filling out a mortgage application, standing at a cashpoint machine and so on. In a similar way, they use their understanding of the immediate context and their past experiences to understand that 'bank' here means a financial institution rather than say a river bank. The frame knowledge that is triggered is clearly context-sensitive and demonstrates how words in themselves only contain a very small amount of meaning. This last point can also be seen in the way in which gesture and other paralinguistic features play a role in enabling the speakers to negotiate meaning successfully.

Knowledge frames also allow us to imagine other states of being, create fantastical and dream worlds and speculate about things that have yet to happen or even are very unlikely to happen. For example, in the following text message exchange, two friends – and fans of rival teams – are talking about an upcoming football match.

A: It'll be tight but I think we win on Saturday. 3-1 I go for.
B: No way, bring your wallet! You'll be buying lots of drinks for the winning team . . .

In this exchange, A projects a future time in which the team that he supports has won the game 3-1. In this conceptual space, his friend is being asked to imagine this as yet unrealised event as a real one, with 'versions' of the two teams having just played a match, and the subsequent reactions of the players and fans and so on. In a similar way, B's response projects a different kind of future event in which the team he supports wins. In his imagined space, A has to buy drinks for supporters of the opposing team rather than enjoy a victory himself. All of this knowledge comes from previous experience, which is triggered as the dialogue unfolds. The imagined 'worlds' that are built up from a minimal number of words show the way in which we effortlessly construct alternative reality spaces that are enriched by frames based on real world knowledge.

4   Grammatical patterns are meaningful in that they provide an idiosyncratic perspective on the events they describe

One of the main principles of cognitive linguistics is that all aspects of the linguistic system are meaningful, and consequently grammatical forms are as important in shaping meaning as lexical ones. A good example of this in practice can be seen in the way in which we can use a number of different grammatical structures to represent the same event in different ways within the clause, depending on which aspect of that event we want to draw attention to.

In English, three of the ways by which the scene in Figure 3.3 can be presented are

1   The man smashed the window
2   The window was smashed by the man
3   The window was smashed

In the first, the active voice is used, which assigns prominence to the agent of the action (the man) through positioning him as the subject of the clause. In this instance, the

Figure 3.3 The man smashed the window/the window was smashed (by the man)

focus emphasises that he is very much to blame. By contrast, in the second, the agency of the verb process is defocused by means of the use of the passive construction. Since 'The window' is positioned at the front of the clause, attention is drawn primarily to its state rather than to the agent responsible for the action. The revealing of agency in this case is postponed until the end of the clause, and blame is downplayed to some extent in comparison to the first example. In the third example, the agency is downplayed to the extent that it is omitted and receives no attention whatsoever in the clause. These constructions all offer different ways of expressing the same state of affairs and impose a certain way of looking at an event influenced by the kind of prominence that a speaker wishes to attach to the scene. Since the grammar then organises the event linguistically in the same way as our visual systems organise scenes into prominent and backgrounded parts, the choice of one grammatical form over another is significant, meaningful, and in a the context of discourse, motivated. Any change from the active to passive voice can be viewed as more than just a simple transformation since any reconfiguration of the grammar implies a different ideological as well as perceptual point of view.

5   We conceptualise, understand and explain the abstract through the concrete

In traditional grammar, metaphor is viewed simply as a literary trope that has no relevance to or use in the study of 'everyday' language. By contrast, cognitive linguistics views metaphor as an important ubiquitous phenomenon by which we organise and understand complex abstract concepts in terms of more physical ones. This represents another example of the important connection between the social and physical world we inhabit and the ways in which we use language to present our experience.

As I explained earlier, expressions such as 'I'm on a real high' or 'I'm feeling low', which are related to states of being and emotions, rely on explaining one kind of area of knowledge in terms of another. In these examples, the more abstract concept (happiness or unhappiness) can be viewed as systematically organised around the more physical concept of vertical orientation (UP versus DOWN), which is motivated by the nature of our bodies and the ways in which they exist and function in their spatial environment. In fact, these UP-DOWN spatialisation metaphors (Lakoff and Johnson 1980: 14) can be found in a number of linguistic realisations, all of which are motivated by distinctive physical bases. Some of these are summarised in Table 3.1.

Another straightforward example of the ubiquitous nature of metaphor can be seen in expressions that capture the essence of life as a kind of journey, understood in the physical sense of moving spatially and temporally along a path. This way of representing the abstract (life) in concrete terms (the journey) is evident in expressions such as 'I'm getting on with my life', 'I'm on the way to success' and in advertising, such as that in Figure 3.4, where the concept of a career is viewed in terms normally reserved for describing a physical journey.

All of these demonstrate that our ability to conceptualise the abstract is grounded in a coherent and organised system motivated by and reflecting our interaction in the spatial and physical world.

Table 3.1 Spatialisation metaphors, from Lakoff and Johnson (1980)

Metaphor	Examples	Basis linked to physical action and environment
Being conscious is up	Wake *up*!	Humans sleep lying down and stand up when awake
Being unconscious is down	He *fell* asleep	
More is up	My income *rose* last year	If you add more objects to a pile, the level goes up; if you take them away, the level goes down
Less is down	If you're too hot, turn the heat *down*	
High status is up	She'll *rise* to the top	Status is linked to power and physical power is linked to being physically bigger (taller) than another person
Low status is down	He's at the *bottom* of the social hierarchy	

Figure 3.4 Metaphor of life and career as a journey in advertising
Source: http://imuturn.com

6   Language is 'usage-based', learnt through experience and situated in real purposes and motivations for use

A final important cognitive linguistic principle is that language cannot be considered outside of the context in which it occurs, and is always motivated by the social and cultural dimensions within which people communicate and negotiate meaning. Although the social dimension of language is a major part of systemic functional linguistics, cognitive linguistics additionally proposes that linguistic form comes both from the way that we conceptualise experience as part of our unique embodied nature and from repeated use in social interactions that over time conventionalises structures and expressions. In cognitive linguistics, the inherent basis of language is both cognitive and social.

This social aspect of the discipline shares the view of systemic functional linguistics that language use is a matter of choice within a system of conventions, with competing ways of representing that experience open to the individual language user in the context of the particular needs of the language event. Equally, its cognitive aspect can be seen in my earlier discussion of the difference between using the active and passive construction. Here, it is possible to explain the difference at a schematic level (whether agency is foregrounded and given prominence or not), and at a more structural level by viewing the grammar as a kind of meaningful template in its own right, experientially based and the result of a specific, contextually informed and motivated decision-making process on the part of an individual user.

The potential value of cognitive linguistics to teachers

So why should teachers be interested in cognitive linguistics? What it might offer to them that is different from traditional and functional approaches? What advantages could it have in the classroom? And how might it be useful in a way that isn't confusing and too difficult for both teacher and student?

At this stage, it would be useful to distinguish between what Carter (1982: 8) calls 'teaching linguistics' and 'having linguistics as a foundation for classroom language teaching'. The aim of the rest of this book is not to persuade readers that sixth form-ers (nor indeed younger or older students) should necessarily be studying cognitive linguistics as a branch of linguistics itself. Instead in the remaining chapters, I hope to offer ways in which teachers can use some elementary principles of cognitive linguistics, such as those I have just discussed, and those I will discuss in more detail in future chap-ters, as ways of teaching students about language structure, grammar and meaning in richer and more pedagogically sensitive ways. Of course, that process will provide a 'foundation' that is cognitively orientated but, as I hope to demonstrate, much of this will naturally fit in with good practice and knowledge about teaching and learning.

One of the primary and attractive benefits of a cognitive approach lies in the fact that cognitive linguistics itself, as a way of thinking about language, offers a kind of psycho-logical dimension and reality that other models do not necessarily have. As I have mentioned previously, the fact that cognitive linguistics places equal emphases on the mental, the experiential and the social is attractive as both a model of communication and in the context of the classroom. It offers a way of focusing on language in use but with some recourse to a cognitive architecture; consequently, language is not just only viewed as a response to social need but also as fundamentally driven by the ways in which we operate as humans. Since the way in which we view and understand the world is dependent on our species-specific bodies, an understanding of the potential to use that unique orientation and the natural movements that accompany it is a fundamental part of any pedagogy that is cognitively informed. Since meaning itself is derived from our understanding of physical experience, it would seem beneficial for the teacher to promote learning and teaching activities that build on this, and use the body in mean-ingful ways. This kind of physical and experience-based pedagogy (*embodied learning*) is informed by how the mind organises and stores concepts (*embodied cognition*). I address these fully in Chapter 4.

Grammatics and tools for learning

Cognitive linguistics offers a way for teachers to draw on the physical and experiential bases of meaning in the design and delivery of classroom activities, and in particular the use of learning and teaching strategies and methods that make use of the body as a powerful semiotic resource. The discipline offers a way of combining the experiential and the conceptual into a coherent pedagogy, building from the assumption that if language and meaning are embodied then it would be advantageous for teachers to think of their learning activities in these terms. Put this way, these ideas become impor-tant tools *per se* by which teachers can plan lessons, and by which students can make sense of the nature of language and patterns in texts they come across.

This type of pedagogy also can easily be aligned to two important theoretical posi-tions. First, Halliday (2002) makes an important distinction between learning how to use a language and an analysis of that language in use in the terms *grammar* and *gram-matics*. In his terms, grammatics becomes the study of the phenomenon (grammar) rather than the phenomenon itself, in the same way that language (the phenomenon) is distinguished from linguistics (the study of the phenomenon) (Halliday 2002: 386). While the former is in the majority of cases learned unconsciously as part of general development, the latter is one of conscious retrospective meta-reflection that primarily is developed in educational settings and contexts. The explicit study of the operations of language that grammatics involves becomes an opportunity for the teacher to move beyond seeing it as a tool to facilitate simple descriptions of structure or of series of rules – it becomes 'a way of using grammar to think with' (Halliday 2002: 416). The grammatics of cognitive linguistics provides a very clear kind of inherent 'grammatical logic' (Halliday 2002: 416) for the classroom teacher that allows teachers to readily adopt its principles as a vital planning resource, and a way of thinking about pedagogy. This grammatics of cognitive linguistics is outlined in detail and exemplified in Chapters 5 and 6.

The second position is the theory of *social constructivism*, most notably exemplified in the application of the work of Vygotsky, and in particular his concept of *mediation* (Vygotsky 1987). Vygotsky argues that our interaction with the world is never direct but is always mediated by tools that enable the movement from lower functioning, such as basic perception, and memory to higher functioning, such as completing complex tasks and engaging in social interaction. Vygotsky argues that these tools are both psychological and culturally determined resources such as language, mnemonics, counting systems and maps, which all function to support cognitive development in the same way as when we use physical tools to undertake material tasks, such as using a car to get from point A to point B. Through a process involving interactions with others, learners internalise these tools or resources and are consequently able to use these independently in a variety of appropriate contexts.

In this way, education can be understood as a process of providing students with tools or resources and enabling them to master these through providing structured activities and support, and opportunities for them to engage in interaction both with their peers and teachers. Viewed in this way, any descriptive model of grammar might be seen as a tool with which to develop the higher-order skills of meta-analysis. Indeed Vygotsky himself had detailed how grammatical knowledge – in his terms close to the hallidayan notion of grammatics – could be responsible for developing more conceptualised and higher abstract levels of thinking (1987: 180). A cognitive linguistic approach offers the potential to be a richer and more meaningful kind of tool, which naturally lends itself to interactive learning tasks, and is, when understood, a better linguistic and conceptual resource for both reflective and analytical work on the nature and functions of language.

Terminology and metalinguistic awareness

Teachers' and students' metalinguistic awareness has been one of the recurring matters of debate about the value and achievable success of language and grammar teaching. Myhill (2000) explored the grammatical knowledge of both a group of PGCE trainee teachers and a group of Year 8 students, and found three types of common misconception. In the first, anxiety and confusion over terminology, often acquired from teachers or textbooks, resulted in either simplistic or partial knowledge regarding word classes and their functions, such as a verb being given the restricted definition of a 'doing word', or in an over-emphasis on prescriptive rules, such as not to begin a sentence with a conjunction. Myhill argues that this kind of limited learning is typical of a terminology-driven approach where the 'definition seems to be more important than the metalinguistic feature it describes' (Myhill 2000: 156). In the second and third types of misconceptions, errors were typically a result of striking and important limitations in the conceptual understanding of a grammatical concept or structure particular to English, or were due to the cognitive demands placed on both the students and trainee teachers in learning a metalanguage itself. These were seen in examples where teachers and students struggled to understand the ability of words to shift class depending on their role and function in a clause, the conceptual difference between abstract and concrete nouns, and the rules and principles of subordination in multi-clause structures (Myhill 2000: 156–159). In all of these examples, it is possible to view these misconceptions as a consequence of the lack of a suitable pedagogy to both understand the conceptual basis of grammar and language in its abstracted forms, and explore those aspects in instances of real discourses and texts.

By contrast, a striking feature of the pedagogical model I am suggesting is the value it attaches to, and the emphasis it places on being led by concepts rather than terminology. This places the model at an advantage over models such as systemic functional linguistics that require a complex metalanguage, even for analytical work at the most elementary level. Where there is terminology to be learned, it is done so in a way that ensures that conceptual understanding is firmly in place first. It subsequently differs from the 'here's the term, now explore it' pedagogy that typifies traditional grammar approaches, and is in line with conventional thinking in psychology and the learning sciences about the acquisition of metalanguage (Bruner 1983) and the ways in which new knowledge is assimilated into existing structures (Willingham 2010). In the case of the latter, a cognitive linguistic pedagogy provides opportunities for students to build up a schematic set of principles for concepts such as modality, construal, metaphor and deixis to which additional layers of terminology can be easily applied.

Finally, cognitive linguistics sees communication in broad terms that stress the importance of both human cognition and social interaction. It emphasises both the importance of meaning, and the ways in which grammatical choices are inherently encoded with meaning potential. By stressing the notion of linguistic choice, which is both available to users but constrained by context, it presents itself as a genuinely attractive descriptive pedagogical grammar. The notions of encyclopaedic and embodied knowledge that I discussed earlier in this chapter highlight its potential to allow students to explore the subtleties and nuances of discourse events and communicative acts in a variety of ways that I explore in the next chapter as *embodied learning activities* (ELA).

Taken together these represent a set of principles for a contextualised and embedded grammar pedagogy that is developed in the following chapters. These are detailed below and based on Carter (1990: 4–5).

1   It is situated in a real text and explores language in use rather than being geared towards merely feature-spotting, the naming of parts and gap-filling exercises.

2   It builds on what students already know about language.

3   It gives them exposure in exploring language before analysing its use and effects in more conscious detail.

4   It leads naturally onto a functional and critical kind of discourse analysis, looking at the motivation and ideology behind language choices.

5   It introduces metalanguage in context and when conceptual learning has taken place

6   It is experiential, student-centred and motivational.

To this list I would add a seventh.

7   It promotes a way of thinking about language that stresses the link between inter-action in the physical world and linguistic realisation. It therefore opens up the potential for a whole new way of thinking and learning about language using visual representation, gesture and movement.

Conclusion

One of the fortunate consequences of looking at grammar and language teaching in a different way is that many of the old values and judgements that accompanied teaching can simply be disregarded. These include over-emphases on either form or meaning at the expense of the other, anxieties about terminology and notions of correctness and debates about justifying the study of language itself. It also steers grammar teaching naturally away from drills and repeated exercises in naming of parts to a more concep-tualised pedagogy that views grammar in the hallidayan and vygotskyan senses as a key resource for the teacher to think with and the student to act with. This will hopefully promote a richer, livelier, more exciting, more interactive and better educational expe-rience for students. One of the many criticisms aimed at formal grammar teaching was that it failed to be enjoyable and interesting for learners (Elley *et al.* 1979: 3). One of the challenges for those who value the role and contribution that linguistics can make to English teaching is to make language work relevant, valid and stimulating again: a different and better approach can achieve this.

However, there are some caveats and some questions for teachers to think about. As Halliday (1967), writing about his own functional grammar as a pedagogical tool, remarks simply transferring a new set of parameters and terms onto existing classroom methods is doomed to fail. So while this chapter and Chapter 5 focus on some cogni-tive linguistic principles and theories, there is clearly a need for some additional exploration of how these principles might be of use in the designing of classroom activ-ities. In the next chapter, I address this concern by returning to the central notion of embodied cognition, mapping out the concept of the embodied learning activity in exploring the potential of the body as a powerful tool of meaning making in the classroom and suggesting ways that teachers can use this to structure activities and support learning.

I should also stress that what I have been outlining and will develop in the following chapters is not presented as either an effortless solution to classroom practice or a magic wand that will lead to an overnight improvement in students' abilities to read, write or analyse language effectively. As with all teaching methods and strategies, it will take time, experimentation and personalisation. In the following chapter, I do draw considerably on the notion of embodied cognition as a theory that should be of interest to educators, and refer to a significant and convincing body of authentic classroom work that utilises and validates this in practice. However, there is still much to be done despite some promising established practice in the teaching of English to speakers of other languages. Here, cognitive linguistics is rapidly growing as a pedagogical theory, and there is empirical evidence of the benefits of using it as a framework to support language learning. Despite the differences between this context and the classroom of the native learner in the secondary school, there is a clear motivation for exploring the potential of the discipline to offer something meaningful and beneficial in a native learner context. Indeed as Ronald Langacker, debating the value of his own model of *Cognitive Grammar* in the second language classroom, suggests:

> I cannot help thinking, however, that the cognitive linguistic view of language is a matter of universal interest, and that its conceptual descriptions of linguistic phenomena are sufficiently natural and revealing to be widely appreciated. In some form I can imagine these ideas being an integral part of general education or **first language instruction**.
>
> (Langacker 2008a: 29, added emphasis)

Further reading

Crystal (2010) gives an overview of the different models and traditions of grammar. Chomsky (1998) is a good collection of key principles and theories in the generative tradition. In the context of education and schools, Collerson (1997) provides a useful overview of traditional, structural and generative grammars as well as a range of activities that utilise functional approaches, while Hancock and Kolln (2010) draw on debates in curriculum and pedagogy in the US to explore the relative merits of various different approaches. Both the rhetorical grammar of Kolln and Gray (2012) and the meaning-centred grammar of Hancock (2005) are influenced by Halliday's systemic functional linguistics. The most comprehensive account of the functional tradition is Halliday and Matthiesen (2013), and the most accessible is Thompson (2013). There has been a wealth of writing on the value of systemic functional linguistics in the classroom. Williams (1998), French (2010) and the collection of papers in Unsworth (2005) are well worth reading. The best introductions to cognitive linguistics are Ungerer and Schmid (2006) and Evans and Green (2006). The potential of cognitive linguistics to influence pedagogy and practice in the second language classroom is given book-length treatment in Holme (2009), Littlemore (2009) and Tyler (2012). The latter devotes a substantial amount of time to reviewing experimental evidence of the value and usefulness of using cognitive linguistic approaches. The notion of *grammatics* was first coined in Halliday (2002) and is explored convincingly and in considerable detail as model of thinking for teachers in setting up activities and responding to students' work in Macken-Horarik (2009, 2012).

Chapter 4

Embodied cognition and learning

Embodied cognition

In Chapter 3, I drew attention to some basic principles of cognitive linguistics and some differences between that model of language and others that have been used as the basis for work in the school classroom. In this chapter, I explore the notion of *embodied cognition* in more detail and outline some of its main principles. In doing this, I emphasise the value of a cognitive linguistic approach in the classroom and explain how embodied learning activities can be used by the teacher to support students' understanding of grammatical and linguistic concepts and terminology.

At its most basic level, the notion of embodied cognition refutes the idea that the mind is disassociated from the body, and instead proposes that our bodies' movements through and interactions with their immediate physical environment influence the ways in which our minds operate. It also acknowledges the interactive dimension of human communication by stressing that the ways in which we conceptualise, think and speak are shaped by the fact that our embodied brains are situated in social contexts. Thus both our bodies and their interaction in physical and social space provide kinds of structures from which we organise and articulate our experiences and present our 'reality' of the world. As George Lakoff and Mark Johnson argue:

> Our sense of what is real begins with and depends crucially upon our bodies, especially our sensorimotor apparatus, which enables us to perceive, move, and manipulate, and the detailed structures of our brains, which have been shaped by both evolution and experience.
>
> (Lakoff and Johnson 1999: 17)

One of the primary ways in which embodied cognition manifests itself is in the phenomenon of *proprioception*, which explains how and why we manage to be aware both of our bodies' position in space and the relative position of our limbs, without needing to have them specifically in our visual field (Gallagher 2005). This is evident in our ability to undertake tasks, such as driving a car, where we can maintain awareness of the position of our arms and legs and use them to steer, accelerate and brake, without having to keep our eyes on them and consequently divert our attention from the road. In a more extreme example, if we reach out to turn a lamp on in a dark room, proprioception explains how we are always aware of our hand's position in relation to our body even if we can't see it or the lamp. You can test this out in another way by closing your eyes and putting your hand firstly in front of you, then above, to the left and so on. Even though you won't be able to see your hand, you'll be aware of its relative position to the rest of your body. In fact, under normal circumstances, it's impossible for this awareness not to be present.

As I explained in Chapter 3, the fact that we have a species-specific anatomy provides certain affordances and constraints that affect the way that we conceptualise and use language. One of the ways that this is apparent is in our reliance on internalised structures that are based on spatial relationships to organise the way we understand and explore concepts. For example, our bodies can be understood as types of containers that have 'insides' and are marked by a boundary. This basic *schema* provides a basis for both physical and conceptual relationships to be expressed.

Linguistically a relationship between an entity and the container is encoded through the use of prepositions such as 'in' and 'out'. As I explained in Chapter 3, this allows expressions to have both a functional significance as in 'the water is in the bucket' and explain more abstract concepts that rely on a physical basis to give them meaning; for example, the idea of falling 'in' or 'out' of love. The way in which we rely on bodily projections to structure conceptual content offers further insight into the embodied nature of our minds. For example, Lakoff and Johnson (1999: 34) explain that the front–back orientation of our bodies is important in the way we project fronts and backs onto objects. They argue that for a stationary object such as a television, we understand the front to be the side that we would normally face when viewing, while for moving objects such as cars, the front is understood to be the part that faces the way it moves and in which we travel either as a driver or passenger. In both examples, the projecting of a 'front' and 'back' is based on understanding and conceptualising these objects in the context of our own bodies, i.e. we interact with people face to face, and generally walk or run in a forwards motion so that the fronts of our bodies face the direction in which we travel (see Figure 4.1). The world with which we interact, and the objects within that world, are thus configured in a way so that they are understood through our embodied selves.

Another very basic schema is derived from our body's movement through space and time along a journey from a starting to a destination point. This 'SOURCE-PATH-GOAL schema' (Lakoff and Johnson 1999: 32) extends from our knowledge of our physical movement into more abstract concepts, which are understood in the terms of its inherent structure (see Figure 4.2). As Lakoff and Johnson (1999: 33) explain, this schema has the built-in properties of something moving from a starting point towards a destination along a defined route. This basic structure is derived from the ways in which our own bodies move in the physical world, and provides a knowledge base for understanding the relative meaning of more advanced concepts expressed by prepositions such as 'toward', 'away', and 'along' as relationships between entities and/or events relative to a line of movement (Lakoff and Johnson 1999: 34).

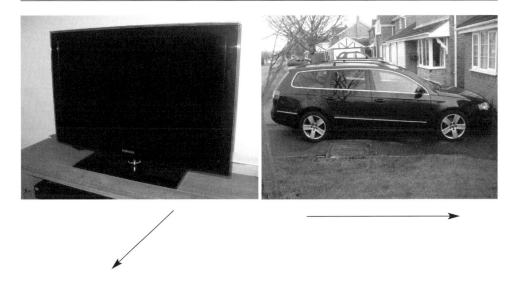

Figure 4.1 Projection of 'front' and 'back' onto objects

Figure 4.2 The prepositions 'towards', 'away' and 'along' based on a 'SOURCE-PATH-GOAL' schema

The CONTAINER and SOURCE-PATH-GOAL schemas are two examples of what Jean Mandler (2004) terms *image schemas*, primitive analogue structures that are based on physical interaction, and from which we understand our conceptual world. Image schemas derive from our early sensorimotor experiences and interactions with the world as young infants. Mandler argues that instances of perceptual information, from vision, touch and hearing, become conceptualised in these schemas that 'hold' basic meanings such as that of containment, the movement of a path through space, the nature of up-down orientation and various kinds and degrees of interactional force. These develop into templates to facilitate first thought and then subsequently speech. Mandler argues that language use is derived from this conceptual basis and linguistic behaviour shows evidence of being underpinned by image schemas.

As an example, she traces how a child might construct a 'path' image schema from her immediate experience with the physical world. She suggests that this originates from infants around one month after birth being able to see the simple movements of objects through space and following repeated instances of this, conceptualising these movements into a more abstract schema of movement from one point to another (a PATH image schema). This schema is inherently meaningful since it is a summative representation of how something operates in the physical world, and is dynamic in the sense that it can be reconfigured based on subsequent experiences (Mandler 2004: 84–85). In this way image schemas can be viewed as providing platforms for future learning to take place. In time, the primitive concept of a PATH becomes more developed and the original image schema can be used to formulate both embedded schemas (for example that paths have separate structures such as beginnings, middles and ends), and further information that is directly based on observed experience. For example, from around four to six months, research has shown that a child begins to be able to differentiate between a path schema that is followed by an entity of its own accord (e.g. a person walking) or one that is the result of external force or pressure from another entity (e.g. someone kicking a football). In this example, the information is 'recoded' into image schemas of SELF-MOTION and CAUSED-MOTION (Mandler 2004: 85), the latter providing the basis of meaning for concepts related to force, later realised in language by verbs of causation and lexical and auxiliary modal verbs.

The ways in which these experience-based physical structures are used to support the understanding of more abstract concepts have been explored in a number of research studies that have examined the ways in which embodied cognition is a part of everyday life. For example, Boroditsky and Ramscar (2002) demonstrate how people's understanding of the abstract concept of time was reliant on their knowledge of spatial experience. They asked the ambiguous question 'Next Wednesday's meeting has been moved forward two days. What day is the meeting now that it has been rescheduled?' to participants in a number of different contexts, among them waiting in a lunch queue and arriving or departing from an airport. The question is ambiguous since it depends on whether time is perceived as an entity we move towards or one that moves towards us, and consequently, the 'answer' can equally be either 'Friday' or 'Monday'. In all of the contexts, the participants' movements just before or during being asked the question influenced their responses. The researchers found that participants who had been asked the question in the lunch queue were more likely to answer 'Friday' the further they had travelled along the queue. In a similar way, there was a clear difference in responses when participants were asked the question at the airport. Those who had just flown in from another location, and who had consequently just experienced moving through space, were more likely to answer 'Friday' than those who were waiting to depart. However, those waiting to depart, were also more likely to answer 'Friday' than those waiting simply to pick a friend or relative up, suggesting that as well as experiencing movement, even thinking about it resulted in a certain way of providing structure to and promoting understanding of an abstract concept.

Similar findings and conclusions were drawn from a series of experiments undertaken by Ackerman *et al.* (2010). They found that the body's interaction with objects through touch provided a scaffolding structure for the ways in which participants responded to a series of questions around social judgements and decisions. Participants were more likely to judge a curriculum vitae as being from a strong and a more interested candidate for an interview post if it was presented to them on a heavy clipboard rather than a light one. In this instance, physical heaviness provided a structure for more metaphorical concepts such as the quality and seriousness of the application (as opposed to a 'lighter' less impressive and less serious one). In another test, participants were asked to complete a jigsaw puzzle immediately before being asked to judge an ambiguously presented conversation between two speakers as being either a discussion or an argument. Those participants whose jigsaw pieces were covered in rough sandpaper consistently rated the conversation as being harsher than those who had completed a jigsaw where the pieces were in a natural smooth state. The implication from this study is that the hand's interaction with the physical world not only provides a structure for conceptual understanding but also influences the kinds of mental operations that are undertaken.

Recent research on the role and function of 'mirror neurons' (Gallese and Goldman 1998) also supports the idea of an embodied mind. Researchers have discovered that watching another individual undertaking a physical action activates a sub-set of the same neurons in our brain that would be 'fired up' as a result of actually undertaking that action. Furthermore, the acts of saying, hearing or reading groups of words related to actions activate the same areas of the brain as when those actions are actually carried out (Iacoboni 2008). In fact, other tests have shown that even listening to others activates the same motor area that is activated through speech (Wilson *et al.* 2004). Mirror neurons provide a good example of how cognition is inherently embodied since they operate by providing a link between the perception of an action, its consequent internal simulation and its subsequent articulation in language. Indeed, the role of mirror neurons as an important facilitating entity in communication itself is also evidenced in their role in allowing speakers in conversations to negotiate turns in dialogue, feed off others' gaze, gestures and posture and contextualise words and meanings precisely without any need for elaborate definitions (Iacoboni 2008). As a consequence, mirror neurons are also thought to be largely responsible for our ability to empathise with others (Stamenov 2002).

Gesture

Mandler's notion of the image schema emphasises the role that an infant's early and exploratory interactions with the physical world play in establishing templates from which further conceptual understanding can be based. In these interactions, the hands are the primary functional tool for young children to navigate the external world both to gather information (e.g. touching things with a view to exploring what they are) and to initiate changes to the environment (e.g. pushing things over). The importance attached to the hands is also evident in the role that gesture plays to support speech in expressive acts, where it has been argued that there is a tight synchrony of speech and gesture operating as part of a single system for communication (McNeill 1985). Since gestures rely on physical movement and the demonstration of spatial relationships relying on physical imagery, they provide a good example of the 'external manifestation of embodied cognition in interaction' (Littlemore 2009: 134).

Corballis (2012) promotes the centrality of gesture as part of an integrated human communication system by arguing that vocal language evolved from manual gestures. He cites the natural potential offered by hands and arms to communicate in four-dimensional space and time, and the ways in which we often revert to pantomime when faced with the difficulty of talking to someone who doesn't speak our language as evidence of the inherent communicative potential of gesture. The importance of gesture can be seen in the way that gesture precedes speech as a communicative tool in children, acting as a kind of scaffold from which vocal language can be built (Corballis 2012: 213). For example, in studying the acquisition of speech in young children, Tomasello (2007) argues that pointing, a specific kind of gesture, is a complex precursor to language and relies on the same kinds of co-operative skills and practices that typify adult speech. Other studies have suggested that the physical mechanics of speech – the movement of the tongue and lips in articulating sounds – means that it should be viewed as a kind of gesture in its own right (Corballis 2002). This *physicality* can also be seen in examples of mappings between physical articulation and meaning. Corballis (2012: 204) for instance draws attention to how in some languages words relating to the second person (e.g. 'you' in English; 'tu' in French) involve an outwards pushing of the lips towards the addressee while those relating to the first person (e.g. 'me' in English; 'moi' in French) involve the lips opening towards the person speaking. Such *phonological iconicity* is often a key feature of poetry, and can be seen in the following lines from Robert Browning's 'Meeting at night', a poem that describes a journey the speaker makes to meet his lover.

> As I gain the cove with pushing prow,
> And quench its speed I' the slushy sand
> (Browning 2000: 43)

In these lines, the speaker's journey across the sea ends as his boat reaches the beach from which he sets off on foot for the final part of his journey. In this instance, the thrust of the voiced bilabial plosive 'p' can be read as representing the sound of the boat pushing through the water, while the run of fricative sounds 's', 'ch' and 'sh' mimic the sound caused by the boat being run into the sand and come to a halt. In both instances, there is a clearly assumed, motivated and iconic mapping between the articulation of sound and meaning.

McNeill (2005) suggests that there are four main dimensions or functions of gesture that are used in conjunction with speech. An *iconic gesture* closely resembles the content of the spoken word that accompanies it, for example, someone playing 'air guitar' or describing scoring the winning goal in a football match by moving his or her head as though heading the ball. *Metaphoric gestures* on the other hand represent 'images of the abstract' (McNeill 2005: 39) such as in a situation where a speaker says 'I'm weighing up all of my options' and accompanies this with a gesture with two hands representing a pair of scales. Here the speaker is using the concrete action of something being weighed using scales metaphorically to articulate the abstract concept of making a decision. *Deictic gestures* are examples of pointing from an originating space towards a physical entity in the immediate physical vicinity or to something that is more abstract such as a thought, an idea or an attitude towards an event or state of affairs. While the former involves the emphasis of something that can be seen, the latter is used to create a reference in the absence of one being physically visible. So, a speaker might say something like 'I was waiting at the bus stop and this woman pushed in front of me just as the bus arrived' accompanied by a hand gesture pointing outwards from the body. The gesture in this instance is deictic since it creates a temporally, spatially and conceptually remote space in which this woman and her actions, although not physically present, can be understood. Finally, *beat gestures* such as rhythmic flicks of the hand either in the air or against objects are used to emphasise certain parts of speech, to signal important moments in narrative such as the arrival of a new character, or to signify aspects of plot and structure. This type of gesture is a largely emphatic one.

One of the most striking ways in which we can see the embodied nature of communication and meaning is through what Müller (2008) describes as the process of *metaphor activation*. Here, a discourse participant uses a metaphorical gesture to activate a metaphor that otherwise might have remained invisible by drawing attention to its metaphorical nature to promote an understanding of the abstract through the concrete. Müller argues that this can have an enlightening effect on communication, drawing listeners' attention to the inherent structure of the metaphor and transforming implicit metaphors into a more clearly defined and foregrounded explanation of a process. One of Müller's own examples (Müller 2008: 205–207) focuses on a speaker reminiscing about a past love experience. In her recount, although speech and gesture largely work together to present content that is metaphorical in nature, there are key moments when the speaker describes the 'ups and downs' of the relationship that gesture provides a finer granularity in terms of meaning. In this case, the speaker

> shows that at the beginning the amplitudes were larger than at the end … It was not just a steady downward movement, but one that contained larger ups and downs at the beginning than at the end.
>
> (Müller 2008: 206)

In this instance the gesture becomes a more prominent part of the speaker's communicative practice and consequently is responsible for activating more of the metaphorical content. In other words, the metaphor is made richer through the use of gesture.

Figures 4.3 and 4.4 show two further examples of metaphor activation. In both cases, the speakers were discussing a recent work initiative that was causing some anxiety among staff. In Figure 4.3, the speaker's gesture accompanied the words 'we're going to have to wrestle with that idea'. The inherently metaphorical nature of her utterance was made explicit and therefore activated through the accompanying metaphorical gesture, which represented the struggle and difficulty that would be involved in making a decision. In Figure 4.4, the speaker's words referring to how staff should abandon the initiative were 'you'll just have to push it away'. Here the

Figure 4.3 Metaphor activation through gesture in 'we're going to have to wrestle with that idea'

Figure 4.4 Metaphor activation through gesture in 'you'll just have to push it away'

metaphorical nature of an idea being an object that can be physically manipulated was made more explicit through the accompanying activating gesture that depicted the pushing away of an object from the speaker's body. In these examples, explicitly activating and drawing attention to the metaphorical nature of words and concepts by using gestures strengthened each speaker's pragmatic force.

McNeill (2005) explains the phenomenon of metaphor activation using the vygotskyan notion of the 'material carrier' (Vygostky 1986), where the gesture is seen as holding meaning through the enactment of its physical form. In this sense, a gesture carries an inherent meaning that is activated in the act of gesturing, and provides both a way of drawing attention to the embodied nature of meaning and a richer communicative utterance. The materialisation of meaning through gesture provides an explicit way of drawing attention to the embodied nature of meaning and to embodied cognition more generally.

Embodied cognition and education

The use of drama activities in English classrooms is of course well established and much has been written about the effectiveness of using activities that encourage a focus on movement, mime and role-play. However, the explicit use of embodied learning in teaching knowledge about language and grammar has received very little if any attention in the context of the secondary classroom. By contrast, and as I have stated at previous points in this book, the application of insights from the notion of embodied cognition has continued to receive good coverage in approaches to second language learning that build on the premise that meaning is derived from physical experience that can be translated into classroom activities that utilise movement and physical imagery. In these pedagogies, speech, gesture and images combine as meaning-making tools for students to use as resources *for learning* and as resources through which they can *express their learning* in the classroom, each with its own particular characteristics and affordances and limitations, or 'functional specialisms' (Franks and Jewitt 2001). In the context of the language classroom, the premise of this book of course is that these specialisms can offer a great deal. In the remainder of this chapter, I explore these ideas in more detail.

There have been a number of studies that have highlighted the effectiveness of gesture in supporting comprehension and in enabling speakers to interact and communicate more effectively (see, for example, Hostetter 2011, Hattie and Yates 2013). Broaders *et al.* (2007) explore the impact of gesture to support learning and teaching more generally by examining how gesture brings *implicit knowledge*, the knowledge that a student has but is unable to articulate or explain, to the surface so that it can be explicitly stated and more clearly discussed and shared with others. The researchers were interested in how the use of gesture as a carrier of meaning would help to students to articulate this implicit knowledge in ways that speech and writing were unable to. Their results concluded that students who were encouraged to use gesture as they explained their learning were not only able to articulate their knowledge in meaningful

ways, but also could support them in developing new strategies for learning and problem solving, and reflect on their usefulness for subsequent tasks and activities. In a
related study, they also found that teachers who used gesture to support their verbal
explanations of mathematical concepts were more successful in relating those concepts
to their students, who in turn were more likely to use gesture to support their own
learning.

In a similar study, Goldwin-Meadow and Wagner (2005) concluded that as well as
being an important resource in supporting learning, the use of gesture decreases a
speaker's 'cognitive load', freeing up space in that speaker's verbal and memory
systems. The researchers found that as gesturing expressed content that would normally
have been communicated verbally, speakers were able to develop their verbal output in
more detail and with greater precision when accompanied by gesture. Interestingly,
their study showed that speakers' abilities to remember lists of words while simultane-
ously explaining how they had solved a previous maths problem were greatly increased
if the explanation was accompanied by gesturing. The evidence suggests that using
gesture can support higher-order tasks that make more cognitive demands on learners.
Educational research has shown that gesture has an important role to play as a kind of
embodied learning, as Hattie and Yates (2013), in a recent overview of the ways in
which advances in learning sciences can support teachers in planning for successful
learning sequences suggest.

> When students gesticulate and use their hands as they speak, their understanding
> of what they are saying can move to a deeper level, and their overall performance
> on academic tasks can be enhanced.
>
> (Hattie and Yates 2013: 141)

Students are often able to demonstrate their knowledge of concepts by using gesture
as a learning resource before they are able to articulate that knowledge in words;
gesture can therefore help make the implicit explicit. This would seem to be a major
factor in the context of learners working on descriptive and analytical work in the grammar of their native language (i.e. in secondary and sixth form English classrooms), since
in these situations students clearly know a great deal about language and grammar (in
Halliday's terms *grammar per se*) but need to be able to express that understanding in
the context of undertaking discourse and text analysis, and in answering questions on
examination papers (in Halliday's terms *grammatics*). So, one of the main challenges
for the English teacher is to plan for classroom activities that encourage students to
make this implicit and unconscious knowledge about how language and grammar operate more explicit. Given that the use of gesture has empirical evidence to support its
efficiency, embodied activities that use gesture as a learning tool would seem to have
great potential benefits. In a similar way to how Müller's research showed that gesture
worked to activate metaphorical mappings used by speakers, gesture could be used as a
resource for supporting the activation of more explicit knowledge about language and
grammar, from which students can articulate that knowledge to themselves, their peers

and their teachers. They could then subsequently develop this knowledge through further work into the kinds of responses demanded by assessment models. The use of gesture and accompanying movements to support learning together form a way of exploring the inherent physical basis of meaning.

An innovative and exciting application of embodied cognition in an educational context using these kinds of learning activities has been developed by a group of physicists at Seattle Pacific University working on an initiative called *Energy Project*. This is a research project that focuses on the potential for embodied cognition to inform the teaching of concepts about energy from which the researchers have devised a series of professional development programmes for teachers using a methodology they term *Energy Theater* (Scherr *et al.* 2010). *Energy Theater* works by asking learners to take on the role of a unit of energy in a given scenario corresponding to a concept in physics, for example, a hand pushing a box across the floor. In taking on the role of the energy unit, students are encouraged to explore knowledge and understanding in a more explicit way, using their bodies to understand abstract rules that have an underlying physical basis. In the box example, the students acting as the units of energy have to co-ordinate their actions so as to provide an embodied representation of the movement of energy from hand to box, and then across the floor showing how various forms of energy decrease and increase in the acts of transference and flow. In *Energy Theater*, students' discussion of the concepts behind energy changes informs their physical actions. In this way the actions themselves become a resource not only for representation but also as an important vehicle for making conceptual knowledge explicit. Furthermore, the interaction and co-ordinated movements promote important questioning and dialogic skills; indeed, an important part and function of these activities is that they promote peer discussion and teaching. Since the activities can also be recorded, they allow students to view their learning process at a later time, to reflect on discussion and decisions they made and to evaluate their understanding. Scherr *et al.* (2010: 1) define the *Energy Theater* practice of working as an example of what they call an 'embodied learning activity'. The work of the Seattle researchers shows the value of embodied learning in the classroom, both promoting the use of the body as an important semiotic resource, and demonstrating how this can be used to teach complex and abstract concepts and phenomena in engaging and pedagogically sound ways. Commenting on the value and effectiveness of their programme, the Seattle group argues that

> ELAs (embodied learning activities) offer a unique combination of benefits. They hold promise for promoting conceptual understanding in physics by taking advantage of motor action in learning, embodied metaphors, perspective taking, and the appropriate status of representations. Furthermore, by promoting the concrete symbolization of abstract ideas and thinking, cognition may be more externalised and thus available for systematic study, especially through the use of video-based interaction analysis. ELAS are naturally life-sized, promoting large-group involvement. Finally, as a free multimedia technology, the human body is unsurpassed; it is representationally flexible, naturally dynamic, conveniently

available, and comes with an extensive suite of tools for symbolization (including gestures, vocalizations, orientations, grips, and so on).

(Scherr *et al.* 2010: 4)

Jean-Rémi Lapaire, a cognitive linguist at the University of Bordeaux, has similarly developed a teaching methodology that utilises gesture and movement this time to teach aspects of grammar. Lapaire's work promotes the use of *kinegrams* (Lapaire 2007) to encourage students to substitute their bodies for grammatical entities as a way of exploring the main aspects of grammar and meaning. A kinegram is an explicitly metaphorical gesture that presents grammatical and semantic structures and concepts in imagistic terms, giving a physical and concrete shape to that which is inherently abstract. It builds on the notion of grammar as a type of performance in which there are specified grammatical entities that have specified roles. The kinegrammatic approach is a way of externalising these roles so that, as with the work on energy, this invisible knowledge may be made explicit and thus built on in further study.

The notion of grammar as a kind of performance or drama is worth some further discussion here. It is possible to understand a prototypical clause as having inherent dramatic potential centred on and round its verb, and we can borrow functional grammar's terminology to label its constituent parts. So, we can label the verb a *process*, entities acting out the verb *participants* and any additional modifying information as types of *circumstance*. An example such as 'The teachers pushed the box across the floor during *Energy Theater*' has two participants each with different roles ('the teachers' are doing the pushing and have agency; 'the box' is being pushed and has no agency), a central process or action ('pushed') and two sets of circumstances ('across the floor' and 'during *Energy Theater*'). In this way, it's reasonably straightforward to see how this clause is dramatic as the participants perform their roles around an action defined in time and space. The relationship between the participants in this type of action clause is one of subordination and manipulation (one participant has more power and thus more foregrounded dramatic potential than the other), and this can be explored using a kinegram that makes this relationship explicit in a concrete way as in Figure 4.5. Asking students to explore this using movement and gesture allows the essence of the clause to be explored in a more up front and systematic way, since students are given the opportunity to actually experience the grammatical organisation of elements around the verb and their relationship to each other rather than just being told about them. I return to this idea in more detail in Chapters 5 and 6 when I explore how cognitive grammar treats the clause as an action chain.

The examples from *Energy Theater* and the work of Lapaire are both instances of what Holme (2012) terms 'actual embodied experiences' since they promote an active movement-based experiencing of structure and meaning. Whereas 'virtual embodied experiences' involve using diagrams and pictures as a way of expressing the physical basis of concepts, but without experiencing them directly. In this case, the space of the page becomes re-configured as conceptual space, into and from which the externalisation of abstract concepts and thus far invisible knowledge can take place.

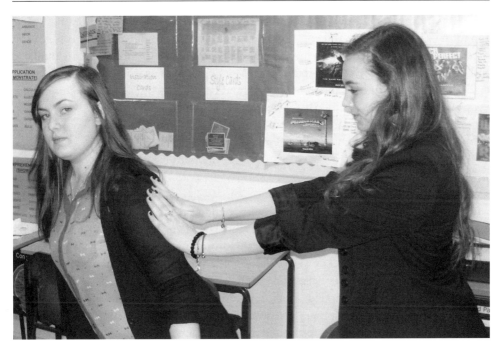

Figure 4.5 A kinegrammatic representation of the relationship between participants in an action clause

The value of using drawings, diagrams and other visual kinds of systems to support teaching and learning has been well demonstrated (see, for example, Wall *et al.* 2005). However, there has been less interest in the role of these activities in supporting the ways in which learners might articulate what they have learnt in the secondary English classroom. There are similarities between drawings and gestures in the way that drawings have been argued to precede speech in a similar manner to gestures (Vygotsky 1986) and a clear relationship between them in that visual representations of phenomena make use of the affordances and constraints of the human body, particularly in its visual–spatial perspective.

Hope (2008) presents a convincing argument for the value of drawings as a pedagogical tool since they represent a mode of thinking that is used widely in our everyday lives, at work, at leisure, in the act of presenting information and in socially orientated and purely imaginative activities and tasks. She suggests that the use of drawings in educational contexts is embedded in two central metaphors where drawing is viewed first as a type of container for ideas, and second as a learning journey that students undertake to explore and develop their ideas. As students draw in response to a learning task, the ideas contained in their initial marks on the page are developed, transformed and integrated into other ways of thinking, building on their own thinking, personal resources or 'funds of knowledge' (Moll *et al.* 1982) from other areas of their life and that of others with whom they engage and discuss. Hope views drawing as a form of both dynamic and explicit meaning in a similar way to gesture. It holds the potential to stand as Vygotsky's important carrier of meaning, and a tool for thinking and externalising. Hope argues that even a seemingly abstract subject such as mathematics can be thought of as inherently visual, and presents a convincing account of how a topic as conceptual as geometry can be taught through asking students to schematise the concepts of size, shape and movements through reference to the real physical world that are articulated through drawing (Hope 2008: 120).

Conclusion

Understanding cognition as embodied allows the teacher to attach importance to gesture and drawing as meaning-making resources and to the nature of grammar as a type of performance, where meaning is derived from physical experience. It also offers imaginative ways for the teacher to exploit the potential of the human body to encourage students to understand concepts and externalise then in meaningful ways. I would argue that these ways of thinking about cognition, embodiment and its potential relationship to teaching awareness of grammar, structure and meaning present opportunities for teachers to explore language teaching in ways that traditional approaches do not afford. They allow students to experience at first hand the embodied nature of meaning and provide a genuine way for externalising implicit knowledge.

In the two remaining chapters of this book, I draw these ideas together to present some teaching ideas that use the notion of embodied cognition and some important cognitive linguistic topics as a way of enabling students to understand and be able to discuss some important topics. In doing so, I draw on the work I have discussed in this chapter to propose a pedagogy for teaching about grammar, structure and meaning. I bring together Holme (2012) and Scherr *et al.* (2010) to propose a series of *actual embodied learning activities* (movement, gesture, role play) and *virtual embodied learning activities* (diagrams and drawings), which turn the physical space inhabited by the body or the page into conceptual space in which meaning can be experienced and explored. All of this is addressed in detail in the chapters that follow this one, but for now I will demonstrate how an example of embodied learning might work in the classroom.

Embodied learning and the semantics and grammar of negation

A way of allowing students to engage with the semantics and grammar of negation would be to ask them to work in pairs on the following examples that contain negated verb processes. As in *Energy Theater*, individuals 'stand in' for conceptual entities, so in this instance one person is the entity attempting to go from point A to point B, and the other is the act of negation that is realised grammatically in different ways. In each case there is a very different socio-pragmatic effect of the construction chosen. This works best if a line, A————B, is physically mapped out in the classroom, along which students can undertake the activity.

1   You can't go there
2   I'm really sorry but you can't go there
3   I'm not sure that you can go there

For each instance, the student in role as negation uses her body to represent the concept, the way that it is linguistically encoded in the example and the possible under-lying reason for that construction being used over an alternative (in essence they provide a potential contextual motivation for that choice). In example 1, the negation is foregrounded by the use of the negating particle 'not' attaching itself to the modal auxiliary verb 'can'. This negates the semantic potential of the verb, shown in the phys-ical restriction in Figure 4.6. In example 2, the negation is similarly encoded but this time there is an added pragmatic force. The fronted clause 'I'm really sorry' acts as a kind of mitigating device, designed perhaps to soften the force of the restriction and to show a degree of empathy. This is shown in the way that the student in Figure 4.7 this time lessens the severity of the restriction and at the same time uses a deictic gesture to present this attention to the other's face needs. However, in example 3, the negation operates in a different way by this time attaching itself to the speaker's own judgement on the reliability of what she is saying rather than a judgement on the ability of the other person to move. The intention is clearly still to restrict movement but this is expressed in a much less certain manner, and is demonstrated in Figure 4.8 by the student's inwards gesture to her own epistemic stance towards the action. In all of these

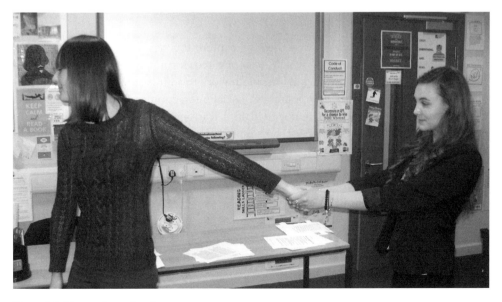

Figure 4.6 'You can't go there'

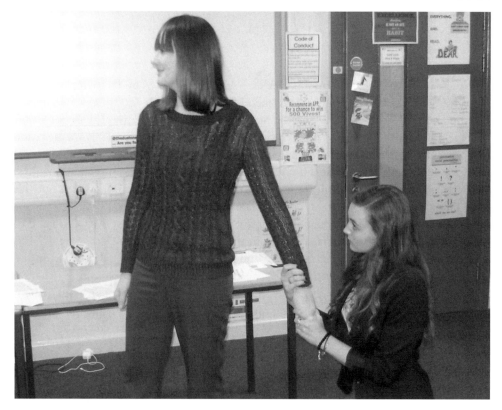

Figure 4.7 'I'm really sorry but you can't go there'

examples, the students' work allows them to explore the ways in which we might use negation and the situations in which one negated form might be preferred over another. It also allows discussion and classroom work to shift naturally to an exploration of other related concepts such as politeness, social interaction and power relationships. Crucially, the students' work is embedded in a learning activity that allows them to experience these phenomena rather than simply being told about them or being asked to consider them in abstract ways. In all of the figures below, the 'negator' is on the right.

Further reading

Lakoff and Johnson (1999) offer a good introduction to embodied cognition, with a range of examples that are linked to linguistics. Gallagher (2005) is a more detailed – although more complex – account from a psychological perspective. Mandler (2004) provides a thorough explanation of the role of image schemas in providing scaffolding structures for conceptualisation and meaning making. The paper by Borodistsky and Ramscar (2002) provides evidence of the ways that abstract concepts are given

Figure 4.8 'I'm not sure that you can go there'

structure by experience. Iacoboni (2008) provides a very readable account of the phenomenon of mirror neurons and their role in human cognition, action and interaction. McNeill (2005) and Corballis (2002, 2012) offer a comprehensive overview of gesture. Müller (2008) proposes the concept of metaphor activation, while the concept of the material carrier is originally from and explored in Vygotsky (1986). Kress *et al.* (2001) highlight the multi-modal nature of communication and the range of meaning-making resources, including gesture, which are brought to and used in the classroom by teachers and students. Broaders *et al.* (2007) and Hattie and Yates (2013) report on the effect of gesturing on making implicit knowledge explicit in the classroom. The latter also includes a useful summary of how teachers might use gesture to support teaching and learning generally in the classroom. Nicholls (1975) and Hamblin (1987) offer ways of integrating movement, mime and role-play into lessons and Fleming (2011) argues for the importance of drama teaching *per se* across the secondary curriculum. Goldwin-Meadow and Wagner (2005) also offer overviews on the synchrony of speech and gesture in the conveying of meaning, and provide empirical evidence to support the thesis that gesture helps to decrease cognitive load. The basis of *Energy Theater* and ELA can be found in Scherr *et al.* (2010) and in Close *et al.* (2010). The

Seattle Pacific University *Energy Project* website www.spu.edu/depts/physics/ EnergyProject.htm has further information on its programmes on teaching physics, as well as resources, training materials and research papers on embodied cognition and the classroom. Ideas on using these kinds of activities to teach science in the context of the UK National Curriculum are presented in Abrahams and Braund (2012). The work of Jean-Remi Lapaire is best accessed through Lapaire (2007), and a good summary of kinegrams can be found at http://dominiquevinet.free.fr/Grammaire_gestuelle/ theory.htm. Lapaire has written a number of textbooks on teaching English to French students using his approach, for example, Lapaire (2006) (in French), which also contains a DVD with demonstrations of students working with kinegrams. Hope (2008) is a convincing account of the nature of drawing and its value in the classroom as an important thinking resource. Ainsworth *et al.* (2011) equally develop ideas on using drawing to support conceptual understanding, While in a comprehensive study of child's development in visual representation, Matthews (2003) offers a fascinating account of how the 'mark-making movements' *vertical arc*, *horizontal arc* and *push-pull*, which form the basis of being able to draw have their origins in a child's first primitive movements in her physical environment.

Chapter 5

Cognitive linguistic concepts for teachers

Scope of this chapter

In this chapter I outline some areas and focuses of language study from a cognitive linguistic perspective and provide some background on these for the teacher. This chapter forms the first part of a pair with Chapter 6, which builds on detail here to present ways in which these ideas might be used to support teaching and learning in the classroom. Both of these chapters use the notions of embodied cognition and embodied learning that I outlined in Chapter 4. The concepts and terms that I describe in this chapter are necessarily selective, and are offered to the classroom teacher as an introduction to some ways of thinking about language, meaning and structure that are informed by cognitive linguistic principles. In each case, I outline the area or focus of study, give some insight into its theoretical concerns and explain how it fits within the discipline of cognitive linguistics. I then provide an example analysis of a short text. In Chapter 6, I develop these ideas within a teaching context to demonstrate how they might be useful in supporting students in their learning.

Figure and ground

In Chapter 3, I provided details of how our perceptual systems organise incoming stimuli and experiences into types of arrangement with certain entities profiled as a *figure* and others as the *ground*. The figure–ground distinction is a major principle in cognitive psychology, and has been used in cognitive linguistics to demonstrate how language assigns degrees of prominence to certain parts of a clause or to a larger textual structure. An obvious way of understanding how this works is to look at an image such as that in Figure 5.1. In this example, you should see either a framed black cross (against a white background), or four white boxes against a black background. In other words, one part of the image will stand out against the other since we automatically assign figure and ground roles to what we see and interpret them accordingly. However, it's impossible to see both at the same time (as hard as you might try): there's always a figure, and always a ground. This is a basic rule of *attention*.

While it's relatively straightforward to see how this figure–ground configuration exists in a visual image such as that in Figure 5.1, written texts also demonstrate this

Figure 5.1 Figure–ground distinction: a black cross or four white boxes?

particular relationship, and are structured so as to draw attention to particular features, aspects or themes within them. Generally parts of a text that tend to be figures will be more clearly defined and described in terms of size, brightness and movement and their position relative to other parts of the text: being mentioned first is always a good sign of a figure. Attention will be maintained on figures if they are continually repeated or referred to and consequently retained as the figure element. Any shift in attention through no longer being mentioned and the emphasis moving to a different part of the text reconfigures the figure–ground relationship. This can have a significant impact on the way in which we asked to engage with and interpret texts, as shown in the example from Ian McEwan's novel *On Chesil Beach*.

> They were young, educated and both virgins on this, their wedding night, and they lived in a time when a conversation about sexual difficulties was plainly impossible. But it is never easy. They had just sat down to supper in a tiny sitting room of the first floor of a Georgian inn. In the next room, visible through the open door, was a four-poster bed, rather narrow, whose bedcover was pure white and stretched startlingly smooth, as though by no human hand.
>
> (McEwan 2007: 3)

In this extract, the couple (later named as Edward and Florence) are afforded attention through being positioned at the front of the opening clause as the referents of 'They' and maintain their position as the figure through the first three sentences as a result of the repeated use of 'they'/'They', which keeps attention on them as objects of readerly focus. However, they are not mentioned in the final sentence and attention is instead afforded to the adjacent bedroom. Here the figure–ground relationship is reconfigured through a series of moves, initiated by the prepositional phrase 'In the next room', which diverts attention away from the current location. Another diverting prepositional phrase 'through the open door' shifts the focus to the bed, before a kind of 'zoom in' draws attention to the bedcover, whose status as a figure is then maintained against the ground of the location and the people staying there, through the detail afforded to it: 'pure white' and 'smooth'. This renewed focus on the bedroom seems significant and could be interpreted in the context of the couple's apparent sexual inexperience and anxieties. The purity of the bed, described as untouched by 'human hand', becomes a symbol of inexperience and anxiety (fusing the object and the lovers it represents), which acts as an important textual and thematic figure in the remainder of the novel.

The example above shows the ways in which figure–ground configuration can position a reader towards adopting a certain interpretation or preferred response to a text. Indeed, exploring the craft of writing, particularly in cases of polemical and rhetorical writing, is a good way of looking at how authors do this. However, there are clearly times when meaning is ambiguous and when a number of interpretations are possible. In these instances, the assigning of figure and ground, often at a more global macro-level, can reside in a reader or listener's individual decisions, own background knowledge and ideological stance. For example, when reading Mary Shelley's *Frankenstein*, readers might feel sympathy and admiration for Victor, or see him as an over-reacher and unattractive in contrast to the Creature and other characters. Interpretative stances such as these are one way that we automatically configure figure and ground status (one interpretation necessarily pushes the other into the background) even at a thematic level. Indeed, the perceptual and bodily basis of this natural tendency to organise is evident in the verbs that I have just used to describe the potential interpretations: *feel* and *see*. Equally, it is possible to shift between these readings and so to re-configure the figure–ground relationship. The relationship between the elements in this scene is a dynamic one, as with attention more generally.

In traditional literary and textual criticism, the phenomenon of textual patterning where prominence is afforded to a word, structure, character or theme is known as *foregrounding*, and as I have just demonstrated in the McEwan extract, can be used to attach significance to specific linguistic choices and justify their interpretative effects. Foregrounding can take place at any one of a number of language levels, and is generally achieved by either establishing patterns, known as *parallelism*, or by making obvious breaks from existing patterns that have been set up, known as *deviation*. In turn, deviation may either be *external* in that it breaks from established generic and linguistic 'norms', or *internal*, if it markedly moves away from patterns that have been set up in the text itself. These can be seen in the examples below.

1   Cut the chicken into strips. Fry and then add the onions and peppers. Put the tomatoes into the pan. [Taken from a recipe.]
    Parallelism at the level of syntax due to the repeated imperative clauses that have a verb+noun phrase structure.

2   There was me, that is Alex, and my three droogs, that is Pete, Georgie, and Dim, Dim being really dim, and we sat in the Korova Milkbar making up our rassoodocks what to do with the evening, a flip dark chill winter bastard though dry. The Korova Milkbar was a milk-plus mesto, and you may, O my brother, have forgotten what these mestos were like things changing so skorry these days and everybody very quick to forget, newspaper not being read much neither. [The opening to Anthony Burgess' novel *A Clockwork Orange*.]
    External deviation due to the way the text does not adhere to the conventions of Standard English grammar and lexis. This initial sense of deviation fades quickly since the novel utilises a consistent style from here onwards.

3   While our rivals are still using tatty sponges and dirty buckets of water, Round-developers use the cutting-edge technology of a reverse osmosis water-fed pole system. [Advertisement for a window cleaning service.]
    Internal deviation since the lexis used to describe 'Round-developers' breaks from the inherently negative with its notions of amateurism, 'tatty sponges', and 'dirty buckets of water' to the positive, technical and professional, 'cutting-edge technology', 'reverse osmosis water-fed pole system'.

In all of these examples, the traditional notions of parallelism and deviation can be described in figure and ground terms, either in the setting up and maintenance of a figure–ground relationship (1) or in the shifting nature of that relationship (2 and 3).

Example analysis

This text appeared in some promotional material sent out by Virgin Media in 2008.

LUMP IT
For many years, the world of entertainment and communications has been in the hands of the people who own it, not you.
LIKE IT
Virgin Media is here to put the world of entertainments and communications in your hands, like never before.

The advertisement attempts to draw a distinction between Virgin and its competitors, and their two respective products. It consists of two parts, each with a verb-fronted clause 'lump it' and 'like it' that highlight two very different emotions and experiences associated with the companies. Our viewing pleasure is highlighted as dependent on this difference, which is understood through the kinds of figure–ground configuration that exist. In the first part of the advertisement, the fronted adverbial 'for many years' is given prominence over the remainder of the clause to give prominence to the length of time that suffering viewers have had to experience poor service. In addition, the first part relies on an image schematic notion of containment, with the service being seen as inside – and controlled by – the TV companies. By contrast, the second part of the advertisement positions Virgin Media as an active figure at the head of its own clause, and an agent in placing a high-quality service in the 'hands' of viewers. In this instance the message is underpinned by a CONTAINMENT image schema in conjunction with movement along a PATH; so here, the act of reading across the remainder of the advertisement involves imagining a dynamic movement that is itself as a strong figure, where Virgin Media is viewed as a prominent agent of action and change, and a facilitator of customer emancipation from the traditional corporations. In fact, this is the kind of profile that Virgin has promoted for itself across its various businesses over the years. This analysis of contrasts that relies on a figure–ground distinction centred round two distinct image schemas is shown in Figure 5.2.

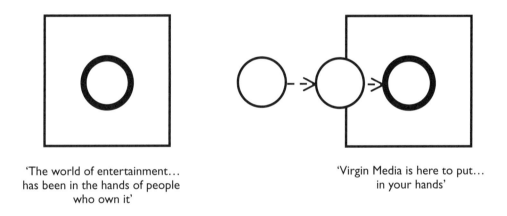

'The world of entertainment…
has been in the hands of people
who own it'

'Virgin Media is here to put…
in your hands'

Figure 5.2 Image-schemas and figure–ground configuration in Virgin Media advertisement

Modality

Modality can be one of the most difficult concepts to teach, yet an understanding of the various forms of and motivations for using modal constructions is empowering for students in both exploring the choices text producers make in given language situations, and subsequently when thinking about making decisions in their own writing.

Traditional accounts of modality tend to define modal forms as instances of either *deontic modality*, concerned with aspects of obligation and permission, *epistemic modality*, concerned with possibility or *boulomaic modality*, concerned with aspects of desire.

A more conceptualised view might extend to understanding modality as either the expression or stance of an individual towards a state of affairs and/or the drawing of attention towards the factual status of an event. So a modal expression such as 'I must go the party' expresses both an attitude (the speaker's obligation to attend the party) and the fact that this has not yet happened, in comparison to the non-modal or *categorical expression* 'I went to the party'. Modality can be expressed through modal auxiliary verbs such as 'must', 'may' or 'could', and using other linguistic forms such as modal adjectives (e.g. 'possible'), modal adverbs (e.g. 'perhaps'), non-auxiliary (i.e. lexical) verbs (e.g. 'like') and modal tags (e.g. 'I guess').

In keeping with its emphasis on the embodied nature of thinking, conceptualising and meaning, a cognitive linguistic approach views modality as a series of patterns centred on the notion of *force* and an understanding of the types of basic movement in the physical world.

Since force is an unquestionably physical phenomenon, it remains an important concept in a discipline such as cognitive linguistics, which stresses the embodied nature of both the mind and meaning. Johnson (1987) argues that notions and degrees of force are ubiquitous in our lives and provide structures for organising our experiences and conceptualisations that can be expressed in language. He identifies the following types of force that we encounter.

1 Force as experienced through *interaction*. For example, when we are in a dark room and bump into a table, we experience the nature of force as one thing interacting and reacting with another.

2 Force as a *movement through space of an object or person*. For example, both a kicked football and a person walking move along a certain path through space. This can be along *a single path of motion* from a *source* to a *target* or *goal*. This particular kind of force can be understood through a SOURCE-PATH-GOAL schema.

3 Force as the result of the power of an *agent*. Things don't move on their own, but are always caused by something pushing on them. This in turn may cause something else to happen.

4 Force as having a *degree of power and intensity* that can be graded and measured along a continuum of strong to weak.

Adapted from Johnson (1987: 143–4)

In Chapter 3, I outlined the notion of an image schema as a basic template for making meaning that arises naturally from the various sensory interactions humans have in their physical environments. I discussed Mandler's (2004) explanation of how these image schemas play an important role in the development of thought and speech in young children in providing inherently meaningful structures into which new knowledge can be assimilated. Johnson argues that modal forms can be understood in these physical terms as instances where people or objects interact with others, blocking or allowing movement and permitting or constraining energy potential. A basic force schema of one entity pushing another arises naturally in very young children through their interaction in the physical world, for example, when something is pushed over. This kind of physical interaction provides a structure for extending into both mental and social operations: expressing a desire to move something; the idea of force as a means of getting something that you want; and for using various forms of modality as politeness markers in interpersonal communicative strategies.

In these terms, the meaning of a modal auxiliary verb such as 'must' derives from the very physical sense of a force pushing someone towards carrying out a certain act. The physical domain is used to understand a similar kind of mental force or pressure being exerted on someone, such as in the example 'I must go to the party'. In a similar way, the meaning of 'may' in 'You may go to the party' can be understood as a restriction being lifted from by a more powerful entity providing permission. Additionally, the meaning of 'can' in an expression such as 'I can go to the party' is suggestive of a potential action, movement or ability that is now available for someone to use.

In their linguistic realisations, image schemas such as those in Figure 5.3 that are based on types of interactive force provide a template for conceptualising different modal forms.

Compulsion: one entity exerts force on another causing movement
e.g. Modal forms: 'must', 'should', 'need to', 'ought to'

Restriction: one powerful entity prevents the movement or actions of a less-powerful entity
e.g. Negated modal forms: 'must not', 'cannot', etc.

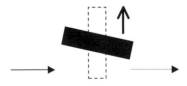

Lifting of restriction: a restriction is lifted by the more powerful entity that allows someone to now do something
e.g. Modal forms 'may', 'can'

Figure 5.3 Examples of the image schematic features of modal forms (adapted from Johnson 1987)

One of the defining features of modal auxiliary verbs is that like force they can be classified or graded in terms of degrees of strength. Degrees of modal force for both deontic and epistemic modal auxiliaries can be placed along continua, highlighting that there are inherently strong and weak modal forms as shown in Figure 5.4. However, as with all choices in language, it is important to consider the influence of contextual factors, including the purpose, and the relationship between participants when thinking about the actual use of modal forms. For example, the use of weaker modal forms does not necessarily imply that a participant is less powerful in any way. It may just be that the degree of force needed in a particular utterance or piece of writing is mitigated by the need to be polite and not threaten face. So there may be very different motivational reasons for a teacher using a weak modal form such as 'You *might* want to improve your essay before you finally submit it' other than just a lack of confidence on the speaker's part. The use of the weaker form (compare to 'You *must* improve your essay before you finally submit it) can be understood and explored in relation to the local context and the speaker's assessment of the impact of his words on the student. The weaker form does have less inherent force, and using the analogy of physical force is likely to have less damaging impact on the recipient, although the overall meaning (you need to do better) is still understood.

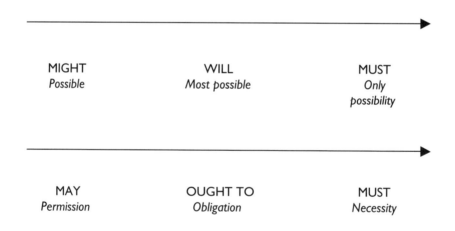

Figure 5.4 Continua of epistemic and deontic forms, weak to strong

Example analysis

This text is part of a letter that was sent by the head of sixth form to all sixth form students in a large secondary school.

To all Sixth Form Students

Please note that tomorrow is the last day for returning any outstanding common room money. Please also note that the following apply to students using the common room as from the 6th June.

1   You must leave PE kit in the locker area. You must not bring any kit into the common room.
2   Tables and chairs are to be left tidy at all times.
3   Music cannot be played during morning lesson time.
4   You may bring food and drink in but please tidy up after yourself.

The context in which this appeared and would be understood is clearly important. The school holds a significant amount of institutional power, and consequently can apply various restrictions on what students can do. The relationship between the text producer and receiver can therefore be considered *unequal* (Fairclough 2002), and this manifests itself in the kinds of linguistic decisions that we see, particularly concerning modality. The text begins with imperative clauses asking students to 'note' main events and dates. These are both fronted with the politeness marker 'please' so as to mitigate their potential to appear too forceful. However, the modal forms chosen afterwards are all infused with notions of force. In section 1, two modal forms 'must' and 'must not' have underlying notions of social force that based on a physical schema of someone pushing something, and applying pressure. 'Must not' is a very strong prohibition, which can be understood in image schematic terms as the restriction of movement through the positioning of a barrier against which no entrance or action is possible. Again, as with 'must', the social and psychological meaning is given shape and definition through our understanding of the physical domain. In addition, the use of 'cannot' restricts the range of possible actions open to the students and positions the school as an institution able to apply a series of constraints on what students are able to do. Even when a 'barrier' is lifted as in 'You may bring food and drink in', it is followed by an imperative, albeit a mitigated one. The modal patterning in this text is that of strong modalised constructions being used. This of course can be viewed in the context of the relationship between text producer and the text receivers, and in the purpose of this text, which is to inform the students precisely what the restrictions are, and to maintain the distinction between more powerful (school) and less powerful (students) participants.

Metaphor

In traditional literary criticism, metaphor has often been viewed solely as a poetic technique, reserved for use in literary texts and other seemingly more prestigious forms of language. However, as I explained in Chapter 3, cognitive linguistics treats metaphor as an important phenomenon in everyday discourse whereby speakers make sense of more abstract concepts by structuring and understanding them in terms of more physical ones. If we look back at the 'Internet Marketing U-Turn' advertisement (Figure 3.4) on page 35, we can see that it relies on a very common metaphor, the understanding of the abstract concept of 'life' in terms of a 'journey', beginning with a starting point, and involving stops, starts and detours, and having a definite end. A more primitive SOURCE-PATH-GOAL image schema, which I discussed in Chapter 4, in turn structures the complex concept of a journey.

Cognitive linguistics treats metaphor as a way of seeing one *domain* of knowledge in terms of another, where an *abstract domain* is given structure and meaning, and is understood in terms of a *concrete domain*. Since concrete domains tend to be derived from things that we directly encounter in the physical world, metaphor can be considered to have a strong experiential basis. Understanding life as a kind of journey involves understanding one domain (life) in terms of another (a journey). In this instance, the knowledge and experience that speakers have of a journey is used to give structure and meaning to the more abstract concept of life. The relationship between the domains 'life' and 'a journey' is understood as an example of a *conceptual metaphor* (in conventional conceptual metaphor notation the metaphor is indicated in small capital letters in a X IS Y structure); in this instance, we have a conceptual metaphor of LIFE IS A JOURNEY. We can also label these domains depending on the part they play in the overall metaphorical structure. As the more physical notion of the 'journey' is the domain providing the structure, this is termed the *source domain*. In contrast the concept of 'life', which receives structure from the source, is termed the *target domain*. A process of *mapping* provides structure to the target domain from the source domain.

In the conceptual metaphor LIFE IS A JOURNEY, constituent elements of the source domain 'journey' are mapped across to provide structure to corresponding elements in the target domain. In this case, the mapping would be as below in Table 5.1.

It's relatively straightforward to see how the relationship between these domains works. A very strong set of mappings underpins our understanding of life as a starting point (birth), an end point (death) and a series of episodes and experiences in-between.

Table 5.1 Mappings in the conceptual metaphor LIFE IS A JOURNEY

Source domain 'journey'	Target domain 'life'
Travellers	People
Starting point	Birth
End point	Death
Events and actions experienced, and places visited	Episodes in life
Distance travelled	Progress in career, relationships etc.
Deciding on a route	Making life choices

These are based on an understanding of a 'journey' as a very primitive sense of movement through time and space from one point to another. Interestingly, this kind of mapping and structure extends to other sub-domains within the broad domain of life such as the ways in which we conceptualise 'big life' experiences and events, such as relationships and careers. In an expression such as 'I went up quickly through the ranks and got promotion', the speaker's career is viewed as a specific kind of movement that combines with another conceptual metaphor UP IS GOOD in a way that conceptualises a career as a particular type of journey along a vertical path, where the higher the position on the path, the better the job, and consequently the more power and better pay the jobholder has. It is clear from this example that whereas a conceptual metaphor provides an overarching structure through which a target domain may be understood in terms of a source domain, the process of mapping allows for any number of actual *linguistic realisations* based on that larger conceptual structure.

LIFE IS A JOURNEY is just one of many conceptual metaphors that underpin the way we view the world and are based on understanding it through our experience of physical interaction with people, places and objects. Kövecses (2002: 16–25) offers the following examples of common source and target domains that can be found in conceptual metaphors.

Common source domains: the human body; health and illness; animals; plants; buildings and constructions; machines and tools; games and sport; business transactions; cooking and food; heat and cold; light and darkness; forces; movement; and direction.

Common target domains: emotion; desire; morality; thought; society; politics; the economy; human relationships; communication; time; life and death; religion; events; and actions.

Although literature can and does rely extensively on varying degrees of metaphorical mapping, it should be clear that thinking of metaphor as simply a literary trope is far too simplistic. Metaphor is also pervasive and an important cohesive device in non-literary, everyday discourse. In the following example of dialogue, two Year 11 students Akbar and Jack are discussing revising for a GCSE examination on *Of Mice and Men*. (.) indicates a short pause of less than a second.

Akbar:	so what you gonna revise for
Jack:	well (.) Slim will come up (.) that's what Mr Jones reckons
Akbar:	yeah (.) he thinks it will be there (.) I bet he's not right though
Jack:	but (.) but I'm not going to risk it this year if it is there
Akbar:	how would he know (.) he's just guessing
Jack:	but he knows the paper really well

What is interesting is here is how the students use the conceptual metaphor LIFE IS A GAMBLE to help co-construct their conversation. This is evident in the linguistic realisations 'Mr Jones *reckons*', 'I *bet* he's not right', 'I'm not going to *risk* it' and 'he's just *guessing*'. The conceptual metaphor extends across their conversation and is used easily and seamlessly by the two participants to help them interact and express meaning. In fact, this kind of negotiated co-construction is typical of face-to-face conversation (see Carter 2004), and here discrete realisations of metaphors are built up from the larger underpinning conceptual metaphor. In the final line of this interaction, Jack's comment that the teacher 'knows the paper well' is a different example of a type of domain mapping. Here Jack is using the examination paper to stand for a wider body of knowledge that his teacher has about the examination system, the specification, the kinds of questions that have previously come up and are likely to come up again and so on. In this instance, Jack uses a specific term to provide mental access to a more general set of affairs. Since 'paper' belongs to the same conceptual domain as the wider examination system, the mapping that takes place is not across domains but rather within one single domain. Here one entity is used to stand for another in the same domain that is closely related. In this case, Jack's expression is an example of *metonymy*.

Metonymy is as equally ubiquitous as metaphor in everyday language. For example, we often use expressions that are metonymic in nature such as referring to parts to stand in for a whole, for example using 'I've got a new set of wheels' when talking about the purchase of a car, or using the name of an author to stand for his or her works as in 'Do you like Shakespeare?'. In this second example, the name 'Shakespeare' provides mental access to other knowledge in 'Shakespeare' domain (in this case his works) that is easily understood. Holme (2012) argues that like metaphor, metonymy is also based on embodied experience, giving the example that in a PART-WHOLE relationship, access is primary based on physical characteristics and qualities, for example in the way that a relationship between the handle of a cup and the cup itself is only understood through the physical act of grasping: literally holding the handle is an access point to the cup itself, of which the handle remains but a part.

Example analysis

This text is a campaign flyer that was produced and distributed during the 2010 UK general election.

> I am your independent candidate, working for local people in this constituency. Unlike the big political parties who put their own interests first, I work for local people. Too often, I have seen our constituents being used as political footballs and time and time again, it's the local people who end up as victims of the power struggle between politicians.
>
> Over the years, I have never backed down from crossing swords with the heavyweights from other political parties. I always put people from this constituency first, and argued passionately and in their best interests. I have fought for what matters to this community and have always let my constituents know of any progress made.

This is a fairly typical piece of political discourse and campaign advertising. It relies on a number of metaphorical mappings to explain an abstract concept of politics in physical terms. The three main conceptual metaphors and their linguistic realisations that exist in this text are as follows.

POLITICS IS A SPORT: 'I have seen our constituents being used as *political footballs*'; 'I have never backed down from *crossing swords* with the *heavyweights* from other political parties' (sports here are football, fencing and boxing).

POLITICS IS A BATTLE: 'it's the local people who end up as *victims of the power struggle* between politicians'; 'I have *fought* for what matters'.

POLITICS IS A JOURNEY: 'and have always let my constituents know of any *progress* made'.

We can take one of these conceptual metaphors, POLITICS IS A SPORT and explain the mapping that takes place between the source and target domains. This metaphor is linguistically realised in the expression 'I have seen our constituents being used as *political footballs*', from which we can identify a source domain (sport – football) and a target domain (politics). The mapping that takes place between the constituent elements of each of these domains can be shown as follows in Table 5.2.

The metaphor works to provide a rich sense of structure for understanding the campaigner's points. He represents other politicians as power-hungry game-players, who in wanting to win have no concern for the consequence of their actions on their constituents. The constituents in turn remain simply passive vehicles for various kinds of actions and events that take place. The use of the source domain 'sport' to structure the target domain 'politics' is common in western societies. In this instance, it allows for an unambiguous point to put across about the campaigner's views on his opponents and the world of politics in general.

Of course, the text above is from the UK and other societies and cultures will have alternative ways of conceptualising and understanding various abstract phenomena. Indeed different individuals in those societies will have their own belief systems and personal histories that affect such conceptualisations and manifest themselves in different ways of thinking with and using metaphors. However, there are some conceptual metaphors that are considered to be 'near-universal' (Kövecses 2002: 165) in that they occur across different languages and cultures as far as can be detected through research. One such conceptual metaphor is ANGER IS HOT FLUID IN A CONTAINER, which has been found to present in a number of diverse languages and cultures,

Table 5.2 Mappings in the conceptual metaphor POLITICS IS A SPORT

Source domain 'football'	Target domain 'politics'
Players on a pitch	Politicians
Footballs	Voters
Scoring goals	Acquiring power
Winning games	Winning elections

including English, Hungarian, Japanese, Chinese, Polish and Zulu (Kövecses 2002). It is likely that this stems from a universal conceptualisation of the body as a type of container, and an understanding of the abstract domain of anger in terms of certain embodied experiences that coincide with the emotion such as an increase in body temperature, blood pressure and pulse rate, feeling pressurised or under stress, all of which are related to physical journey of blood as it flows around the body. Linguistic realisations of this conceptual metaphor such as 'I was boiling over', 'I exploded with anger', 'anger built up inside me' can be found in all of these languages, suggesting that the conceptualisation itself is difficult to explain without resorting to a theory of conceptual metaphor, the experiential basis of meaning, and subsequently the notion of embodied cognition.

Deixis

'Come' and 'go' are both verbs that present types of movement. However, there is a clear difference in their meaning if we imagine using them in a specific context. Figure 5.5 illustrates the difference.

1   **Come upstairs**
2   **Go upstairs**

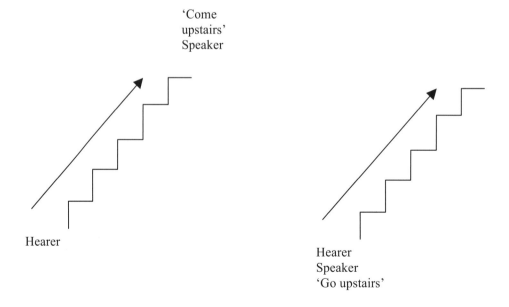

Figure 5.5 Orientation of the deictic verbs 'come' and 'go'

In the first utterance, we would imagine a speaker at the top of a staircase and the hearer at the bottom being asked to move *towards the speaker*. However, in the second, we assume that both speaker and hearer are at the bottom of a staircase and the speaker is directing the hearer *away from him*. Of course these utterances might be accompanied by an adverb such as in 'come here' or 'go up there', which project their movement either towards or away from a particular speaking centre. This idea of *projecting* or *pointing outwards* from an originating centre is the essence of deixis. In the examples above, 'come' and 'go' are examples of *deictic verbs* since they point outwards either towards (come) or from ('go') *a deictic centre*. A deictic centre can be seen as the point of origin of an utterance, which establishes a reference point from which deictic lexical items can be both projected and understood.

Deictic terms belong to one of a number of categories, the four main ones being: *perceptual deixis* (e.g. names and personal pronouns); *spatial deixis* (e.g. adverbs of place such as 'here', 'there', demonstratives showing location such as 'this' and 'that' and deictic verbs such as 'come' and 'go'); *temporal deixis* (e.g. temporal adverbs such as 'today', 'yesterday' and 'tomorrow', prepositional phrases such as 'in two hours', 'in two weeks' time'); and *relational deixis* (e.g. terms of address such as 'sir', 'professor', 'mate', particular registers such as conversational or more formal styles of speech and lexical items that express a writer or speaker's attitude towards a person or event such as 'brilliant', 'terrible' and 'OK'). Each of these both locates a speaker in and projects a position, identity or viewpoint from a particular deictic centre or vantage point.

Because the notion of projection is so important to deixis, texts that make extensive use of deictic terms tend to be those where the positioning of a reader/listener is important in relation to what's happening in the discourse event. In other words, deictic terms build *the context* in which participants communicate. In the following two examples, the deictic terms are an integral part of ensuring effective communication takes place.

1   This is an extract from an audio-guide given to visitors to a farm. The locations mentioned in the running commentary correspond to where the visitor is on the tour.

> To the left is one of the bronze gates that were used by farmers to help contain their sheep. On this gate, you'll see a number of etched markings. These markings were used by the farmers to help them remember the number of sheep that had passed through. Later during the tour, you'll see the place where the sheep were kept. To the right, you'll notice the area where other animals were allowed to graze.

In this example, deictic terms help to position the visitor at a specific location at the farm as she undertakes the tour, acting as *orientational devices*. So, spatial deixis in the form of the prepositional phrases 'to the left' 'to the right' and 'on these gates' is used to point outwards from the deictic centre of the visitor. The demonstratives 'this' and 'these' act as further reference points and as they point to items in the visitor's proximity, these are known as *proximal deictic terms* (in comparison 'that' and 'those' would be used to point to more remote items and so are known as *distal deictic terms*). Finally, a temporal adverb 'later' projects a future time frame when the visitor will be able to see the area in which the sheep are kept. Throughout the commentary, the perceptual focus and the deictic centre are maintained through the use of the second person pronoun 'you', an example of person deixis. The careful use of deictic terms is important in this context to ensure cohesion in that the commentary that the visitor is listening to must correspond to the physical location of the visitor on the tour.

2   In this extract, a window-cleaner (S) is talking to one of his customers (P) about some potential work. (.) denotes a short pause of less than a second. Actions are shown in square brackets [ ].

> S: So sir, what we'll do is clean up there [points] and then use the poles to reach the top bits, can you see those?
> P: yes (.) yes so when would you be back after that
> S: three weeks' time if you are happy
> P: yes that's ok for me (.) but I'm a bit worried about er this gutter (.) can you see that bit [points]
> S: that's fine (.) you've no problems with the poles, look at this bit here [shows pole to customer]

In this example, the participants use deictic terms to help create a shared context of reference and a shared deictic centre from which the discourse event takes place. The spatial deictic terms 'there' and 'those' are used by the window-cleaner, in these instances in conjunction with physical gestures. We can assume that because 'there' and 'those' are used when referring to more remote objects (i.e. they are examples of distal deixis) that the window-cleaner and customer are some distance from the 'top bits' they are referring to. By contrast, the proximal deictic term 'this' when referring to the gutter and later the window-cleaner's pole suggests closeness. In both cases the immediacy of the context in which this discourse takes place and the ease with which the participants are able to communicate are established through the use of deictic terms.

Viewed through the lens of cognitive linguistics, deixis is a phenomenon that has a physical and experiential basis. If I utter the words 'I am here today' at this point in time (November 2013), my lexical choices are centred on and project from a particular person (me), place (my desk) and time (November 2013). But, if I say those words in a different place and at a different time, then the words 'here' and 'today' will obviously locate me in, and project me from, a different set of parameters. If instead of me, someone else says those words then the perceptual centre as well as the time and place to which they refer will change again. In reading a text, we can therefore shift between particular *deictic fields*, from one perceptual, temporal or spatial centre to another. The notion of *deictic shifting* (Segal 1995) is based on a primitive notion of movement based on the simple image schemas 'IN' and 'OUT'. In other words, a cognitive or conceptual shift is understood as a physical one, where conceptual movement can take place across one or more deictic fields.

Example analysis

The following example from an online travel brochure demonstrates the notions of deixis and deictic shifting.

> Some of Italy's most famous sights are along the Neapolitan Riviera, a vision of classical ruins, sophisticated towns and the dramatic Mount Vesuvius. Walk among the remains of Roman Pompeii, or voyage across the spectacular Bay of Naples to the picturesque island of Capri or the thermal springs and enchanting harbour of its neighbour, Ischia. The designer shops of the city of Naples and the narrow winding streets of bustling, cliff-top Sorrento provide further diversion, while a leisurely drive along the coastal roads offers an impressive landscape with many a photogenic view. The striking Amalfi coast is also within easy reach.
>
> www.thomascook.com

The initial movement in this text is the most obvious one and involves a reader re-orientating herself spatially and probably temporally away from the current location and time of reading to position herself within the deictic field of the Neapolitan Riviera from which the remainder of the text operates. Further movement progresses as the reading of the extract continues, marked by a run of prepositional phrases '*among* the remains . . .', '*across* the spectacular bay . . .' and '*to* the picturesque island of Capri . . .' As I argued in Chapter 4, prepositions and the phrases within which they act as heads are given structure and meaning through a SOURCE-PATH-GOAL image schema, which is based on a primitive sense of bodily movement (Mandler 2004). In this example, the deictic centre moves as we scan and re-orientate ourselves from a particular vantage point from which to understand the deictic co-ordinates of the text. Indeed the 'closeness' we feel to the location – and probably the more likely we are to be tempted by the brochure's claims about the landscape – in terms of reading this text can be accounted for by its use of spatial deixis, as well as the additional relational deictic terms, which act to anchor a specific attitude and point of view to the described events. In this instance, we are asked to project and position ourselves as readers to see the '*enchanting* harbour', 'the *narrow winding* streets' and 'the *impressive* landscape with many a *photogenic* view'. Finally, the fact that we are told that the Amalfi coast is 'within easy reach', implies a further act of positioning where we understand the location being described as literally close to our bodies. Proximity in this instance is understood in the context of our own experience of being able to touch objects and entities close to us. The reality is of course that the Amalfi coast is only within 'easy reach' in the world of the Neapolitan Riviera, not the kitchen, lounge or travel agent's office from where we might be reading this text!

The example above and its associated projections show how the concept of deictic shifting can also be understood through the conceptual metaphors HERE IS NOW and HERE IS CLOSE, where any deictic centre from which reading takes place is understood as being in the present time frame and conceptually and physically near to us. The way in which a reader or listener re-positions and projects herself to maintain this sense of closeness is a hallmark of deixis. In the travel brochure example, we can see how deictic shifting can create reading experiences where readers draw on their physical experience of movement in the world to understand what is going on. Indeed the final act of finishing reading the extract and 'returning' to one's 'real world self', initiates a further deictic shift way from the world and the projected version of you enjoying the location and the scenery that has been described in the text.

Clausal action chains

In Chapter 4, I drew attention to how cognitive linguistics treats the active and passive voice not as a simple transformation of structure and meaning, but as an important way of assigning prominence either to the agent of an action (active voice) or the entity or object affected by that action (the passive voice). In the expressions 'the man smashed the window' and 'the window was smashed by the man', exactly the same event is being described but is construed in a different way to give both a different ideological and a different perceptual viewpoint. Viewed in this way, different *construals* assign a different object of attention within the clause as follows.

The man smashed the window: the 'man' is assigned agency at the head of the clause in the active voice, and foregrounded to make him the focus of attention.

The window was smashed by the man: the window, affected by the verb process, and the process itself are given prominence through the use of the passive voice, and foregrounded to make those the focus of attention.

We can also make further sense of these kinds of grammatical patterns using the notion of an *action chain* (Langacker 2008b). Here, grammatical form is understood in terms of a basic image schema from the physical world of forces interacting. As Langacker (2008b: 355–356) explains, an action chain is conceived from our world knowledge of objects moving through space and interacting with each other through forceful contact. Some of these objects supply their own energy to these interactions, while others rely on receiving or simply absorbing it within the chain. We can assign participant roles to lexical items around the verb process that sits at the heart of a clause. In Chapter 4, I illustrated this dramatic potential of the clause using terms from hallidayan functional grammar. In Langacker's *Cognitive Grammar*, participants within a clause/action chain typically play one of the following roles:

an *agent*: an energy source, wilfully undertaking an action affecting others and the head of the action chain;
a *patient*: something that is affected by an outside force and changes in state as a consequence, the end of the action chain;

an *instrument*: something that is used by the agent as part of an action and transmits energy from the agent to the patient.

(Langacker 2008b: 356)

These participants form different kinds of action chain. Returning to the previous two examples, we can reconfigure our analysis of their differences in terms of a series of interacting forces. In the first, 'the man smashed the window', a straightforward transfer of energy occurs from the man (agent) to the window (patient). The agent is afforded prominence through its initial movement and stands out as the figure against the entity it affects. In this instance, there is no instrument explicitly named, but clearly one is implied since the man would have had to have used something to transmit the energy needed from himself to the window. We could add an instrument easily, for example, in 'the man smashed the window with a stone' or 'the man smashed the window with his hand' to show how this energy was passed from man to window. Viewed as a clause, the physical nature of the grammar can be shown visually as an action chain, with an arrow denoting the source and direction of energy. Langacker (2008b: 355) calls this typical transitive clause structure a 'billiard ball model', since as in the game of billiards one entity acts to affect another through some kind of energy release, transmission and subsequent change. This is shown in Figure 5.6.

Figure 5.6 Action chain for 'the man smashed the window'

In the second example, 'the window was smashed by the man', the same scene is being described, but crucially the use of the passive voice either downplays the agency or, if the sentence read 'the window was smashed', deletes it entirely. In a passive form, the patient becomes the clausal subject and the focus of attention is on the process of energy transfer itself and its impact on the patient rather than the agent of that transfer. In Figure 5.7, the focus assigned to the passive voice is shown through the emphasis in the action chain solely on the process of energy transfer and the patient that both absorbs and is affected by that energy – the agency is either downplayed or omitted. This particular grammatical structure therefore draws attention only to certain parts of the event (shaded in the diagram).

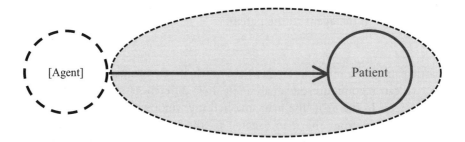

Figure 5.7 Action chain for 'the window was smashed by the man'

There are two points here that are worth mentioning. First, two further ways of expressing the same scene might be 'the stone smashed the window' (emphasis on the instrument but not the agent), and 'the window smashed' (emphasis solely on the end state of the smashed window). The different perspectives thus taken on the same event and action chain can explain the grammatical organisation of each. In our initial typical transitive clause, all three elements (agent, patient and instrument) are present and profiled (Langacker 2008b: 369); in the 'stone broke the window', only the instrument and patient are; while in 'the window smashed' only the patient is. In the examples below, those entities and energy transfers (>>) that are realised linguistically are in bold. In the final example, we can see that neither another participant nor any energy source or trail is specified since the patient is simply the end of the action chain. This explains why a 'perspective' such as this one will be realised as an intransitive clause, and consequently has no object.

The man smashed the window with a stone
Agent (subject)>>Instrument>>Patient (object)

The stone smashed the window
Agent>>**Instrument (subject)>>Patient (object)**

The window smashed
Agent>>Instrument>>**Patient (subject)**

Exemplification adapted from Langacker (2008b: 369)

The discussion above has concentrated on clauses that have verb processes involving concrete actions, and where consequently it is fairly straightforward to see an analogy between the physical world and notions of energy transfer, and the way in which language is organised to describe those actions. However, in many clauses, verb processes denote other things such as states of thinking, speaking, behaving, being and having, where clearly it is more difficult to think in action chain terms. While there are alternative terms within Langacker's Cognitive Grammar to explain these (see

Langacker 2008b for a summary), I will not deal with them here since my attention is solely on action chains, and the section on clauses in Chapter 6 focuses on exploring the differences between and the use of the active and passive voice.

Example analysis

This is an extract from the opening section of a government published report on the 2011 London riots.

> On Thursday 4 August 2011, Mark Duggan was shot by police officers in Tottenham, London. The incident was immediately referred to the Independent Police Complaints Commission. On Saturday 6 August, the family and supporters of Mr Duggan, numbering around 120, marched to Tottenham police station to protest about the shooting. It was a peaceful protest but, later in the evening, violence broke out.
>
> www.gov.uk/government/uploads/system/uploads/attachment_data/file/
> 211617/Govt_Response_to_the_Riots_-_Final_Report.pdf

In this extract, we can identify some clear patterns in the way in which each event has been presented and identify some possible motivations for each construal. First, the shooting of Mark Duggan is presented in the passive voice, with the patient (Mark Duggan) and the process emphasised in the action chain, but with the agent (the police) defocused and downplayed to the end of the clause. This is repeated in the second clause, where although 'the incident' is not strictly a physical event, it is understood as such through an EVENTS ARE OBJECTS metaphor, and therefore can be passed along (referred) in an action chain, where on this occasion no agent is specified. In both of these examples, the de-emphasising of the agent is significant. However, the final two clauses are different since they contain no action chains as such and neither has two participants that interact and transfer energy. Although 'the family and supporters of Mr Duggan . . . marched to Tottenham police station' looks like a transitive clause, it cannot actually be passivised, 'police station was marched to by Mr Duggan's family and supporters' does not work. In this instance there is an agent, but without any explicit suggestion of a violent action and an effect.

The use of the double passive and intransitive clauses are therefore motivated by the report's requirement to sound objective, and not assign blame. Equally, another intransitive clause 'violence broke out' presents a somewhat neutral construal of the events of the evening. Here, there is no mention of an agent, patients or any instruments, and instead the clause merely offers a summary of what happened in a form that states the end product of what is an implied action chain. This could have read something like 'Rioters attacked cars and shops with weapons', but this kind of construction is deliberately avoided. The report more than likely chooses this alternative way of presenting events to avoid explicitly linking any of Mark Duggan's family and supporters to the violence, and consequently being accused of bias. The example thus shows how the use of a particular grammatical construal to present an event is necessarily dependent on specific contextual factors that provide constraints on the choices a text producer can make.

Imagined worlds

One of the most intriguing human capacities is our ability to imagine alternative states of being and worlds very different from the ones in which we live, see and feel. When we read both fiction (e.g. novels) and non-fiction (e.g. advertisements), we transport ourselves into rich worlds that are given substance and vitality through our act of reading. This ability to become consumed into these states so that they appear real is evident when we describe books and television programmes as 'realistic', talk of 'being lost' in a book and describe degrees of empathy with fictional characters and the worlds in which they inhabit. Text world theory is a dynamic cognitive linguistic model of discourse processing that explains how we create these kinds of imagined worlds. It aims to demonstrate how writers/speakers and readers/listeners work together to build rich conceptual spaces using textual detail and their own stores of encyclopaedic knowledge. In text world theory terms, these *discourse participants* share a *discourse world*, which consists of their immediate physical surroundings, their individual and culturally dependent ideologies, memories and desires and the vast array of both shared and personal knowledge they hold. From this discourse world, they co-construct *text worlds*, relying on the words in the text and their own knowledge systems that build those words into richer and personally meaningful conceptual spaces. These text worlds have *world-building elements* that set up their spatial and temporal parameters, populating them with people, places and objects and *function-advancing propositions* that drive the narrative forwards.

For example, when in the discourse world, I read a sentence in a magazine or a book such as 'Yesterday, I got on the train and travelled to London', I automatically construct a text world, located in the past and at a train station, and within that world, project the event of a train journey to London. The world is fleshed out from my real-life experience of train journeys (going to a station, buying a ticket, boarding a train, the journey itself and so on). From this it's clear to see that while my text world will be very similar to those of others, there may be some differences depending on the kinds of knowledge and experiences of trains and journeys I and they have had, and of course their own background in terms of society and culture. Text world theory has what is known as *the principle of text-drivenness*, a kind of safety valve for ensuring that only background knowledge activated by the text is used in the construction of text worlds. So in this case, only knowledge relating to train journeys and travelling to London is initially of any use. Any knowledge I have about football matches, the English political system or the climate of America's Pacific coast will clearly not be triggered when I read this text!

As we read a text, further *world-switches* can occur when the current world's parameters are changed in some way. This generally occurs through shifts in time or place, through modalised expressions that capture a particular point of view or attitude towards a state of affairs, or through more complex constructions, such as metaphor, that demand that the contents of a text world are understood in an alternative way. If my train example continued with 'The journey reminded me of when I had visited my uncle ten years earlier', I would construct a new world, set ten years in the past and involving another journey, this time including the presence of a second character, my (imagined) uncle. In the act of reading, my attention is diverted away from the initial text world to the world switch, which may be permanent, for example if the focus of the narrative was now on the visit to the uncle, or temporary if the memory was only a fleeting one and the narrative then returned to the more recent journey. Clearly, the word 'uncle' could also have associate meanings unique to individual readers as well as referring more generally to a male relative.

Conventionally, text world theory has made use of diagrammatic notation to show the relationships between types of world. This notation is used in Figure 5.8. Figure 5.9 illustrates how initial textual input is supplemented by background knowledge in the building of a rich conceptual space.

As an analytical model, text world theory is a particularly useful tool for exploring the kinds of personal and culturally shared knowledge that readers use to construct meaning, and for considering how this knowledge interacts with textual detail to form rich conceptualisations. It also provides a useful way of exploring the kinds of deictic shifts that readers may have to undertake in a reading experience, and of contrasting and exploring the effect of various types of movements by which readers are asked to track aspects of and changes in time, space and modality.

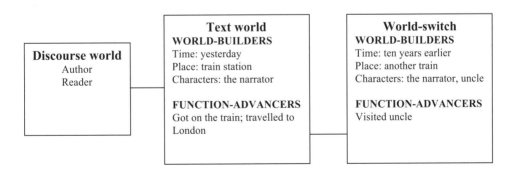

Figure 5.8 Discourse world, text world and world-switch for 'Yesterday I got on the train and travelled to London. The journey reminded me of when I had visited my uncle ten years earlier'

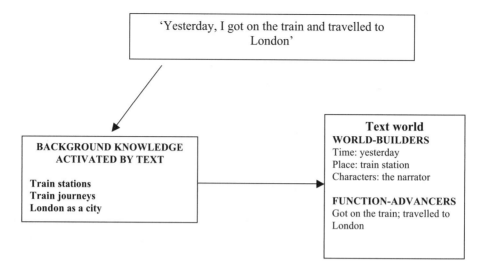

Figure 5.9 The role of text-activated background knowledge in text world formation

Example analysis

The following example, from the opening of Hanif Kureishi's novel *Intimacy*, illustrates how text world theory can account for the rich interpretative significance of a text's conceptual layers. In this extract, the narrator, Jay, reveals that he is going to leave his partner and their children. In the space of just under 100 words, the reader is asked to follow Jay's narrative and position him or herself in each of the as yet unrealised conceptual spaces that are set up.

> It is the saddest night, for I am leaving and not coming back. Tomorrow morning, when the woman I have lived with for six years has gone to work on her bicycle, and our children have been taken to the park with their ball, I will pack some things into a suitcase, slip out of my house hoping that no one will see me and take the tube to Victor's place. There for an unspecified period, I will sleep on the floor in the tiny room he has kindly offered me next to the kitchen.
>
> (Kureishi 1998: 3)

In reading this text, the reader first has to position him or herself deictically outside of the current reading stance and enter a fictional world set up by the narrator's voice, which provides the orientating centre for the narrative. There is an indication of time 'night', and some indication of the narrator speaking. The fictional world is further fleshed out through a world-switch that moves forward in time and then a series of function-advancers that provide details of when the narrator waits until his wife and children have left before packing his things, leaving and going to his friend Victor's house. This future time carries on indefinitely, 'for an unspecified period', and further details of where Jay will be staying are provided 'the tiny room . . . next to the kitchen'. As we read and interpret the extract, we do so by using our encyclopaedic knowledge of relationships (what happens when partners split up), people (why Jay might choose to go to stay at his friend's house), and objects (bicycles, balls, parks, suitcases, the tube etc.) to create a rich fictional world that is resonant with meaning, some of which will be idiosyncratic but a large proportion will be shared by the majority of readers. The knowledge that we rely on can be *actual knowledge* about the world that we bring to the reading experience, *fictional knowledge* about the characters (one is called Jay, one Susan), and an evolving *internal knowledge* that is built up through reading and navigating the world of the novel to support an interpretation, such as knowledge about Jay and Susan's relationship and their feelings for each other.

The movements across time and space also provide a particularly stark way of conceptualising Jay's relationship. The initial stability of the family home (Jay and Susan's relationship) becomes a fragmentary collection of various world-switches distinct in time and space from the original text world. By the end of the paragraph, we have moved from the original description of the family unit to a spatial redistribution of the family that will take place on the following day: Susan (work); the children (at the park); and Jay (at Victor's house). Presented in explicit diagrammatic form in Figure 5.10, the impact of this reconfiguration, and the likely thematic concerns of the remainder of the novel are clearly highlighted.

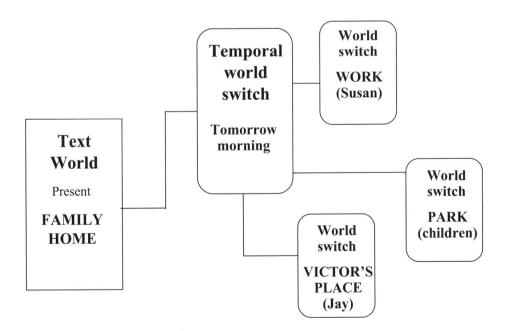

Figure 5.10 The spatial distribution of the family in the opening chapter of Intimacy

Text world theory is a good model for interpreting contrasts between conceptual states, and for exploring the degrees in which the knowledge that readers have is used in conjunction with textual detail to set up rich fictional worlds. In Chapter 6, I explain how teachers might use the principles of text world theory to enable students to explore the genre of advertising, which relies both on the setting up of alternative worlds as contrasting and competing imagined spaces to the 'real world', and to consider the sorts of knowledge that they and other readers make use of – and text producers to some extent rely on – when reading advertisements.

Conclusion

The models discussed in the sections above all provide some detailed description of some concepts and models that sit within the broad discipline of cognitive linguistics. These offer alternative ways for teachers to think about how some areas of language study are considered in cognitive linguistic terms, and as such represents a powerful way of thinking about language itself. For teachers, it provides a view of language that is extrinsically linked to the embodied nature of meaning and therefore offers opportunities for this to be exploited through a certain type of pedagogy and a certain type of classroom activity. In short, it provides a good example of Halliday's *grammatics*. In the following chapter, I build on each of the sections and their concepts discussed here to demonstrate how teachers can exploit this as 'a way of using grammar to think with'.

Further reading

Stockwell (2002) offers an excellent overview of figure and ground, deixis, metaphor, and text world theory from a cognitive linguistic perspective, and uses them to analyse examples from literary texts. Ungerer and Schmid (1996) give a more narrow linguistic coverage to figure and ground, metaphor and action chains. Stockwell (2009) explores the notion of literary *texture* through the notion of attention, while Bate (1997) provides an intriguing discussion of the 'aspectuality of truth' a version of the figure–ground phenomenon in the study of interpreting Shakespeare's plays. The notion of foregrounding is originally in Havránek (1964) and discussed in detail in Leech and Short (2007). Modality is covered thoroughly in Palmer (2001). The idea that modal forms are can be understood via notions of force dynamics is also explored in Talmy (1988), and Sweetser (1990). Other accounts of modal force and gradation can be found in Halliday and Matthiesen (2013), and Hodge and Kress (1988). The best accounts of metaphor are in Lakoff and Johnson (1980), Lakoff and Turner (1989), Kövecses (2002), and Semino (2008). Lakoff (1992) writes extensively about metaphor and political discourse. Geary (2012) is a very accessible book that examines metaphor in a range of types of discourse. The concepts of deictic shifting and deictic shift theory are outlined in Segal (1995). Tyler (2012) exemplifies the HERE IS NOW metaphor in relation to her own research on verb tenses and politeness strategies. Langacker (2008b) outlines the notions of action chains and participant roles. These are also given good coverage in Ungerer and Schmid (1996). The original text world theory model is covered in Werth (1999), but the most recent and best account is in Gavins (2007). Giovanelli (2010) explores the pedagogical potential of text world theory in the A level English classroom, and Giovanelli (2013) provides a book-length study of how the model can provide a systematic account of reading a canonical poet (John Keats). Doležel (1998) outlines the concepts of *actual*, *fictional* and *internal* knowledge, and how we use these in the act of reading.

Chapter 6

Embodied learning activities for the classroom

Scope of this chapter

In this chapter I build on the theoretical principles outlined in Chapters 3 and 4 and the background concepts outlined in Chapter 5 to present a series of embodied learning activities that teachers can use with their students to promote an understanding of some key aspects of meaning, structure and language. These are outlined in detail with ideas for structuring learning activities and some comment on the kinds of textual and contextual features that teachers and their students might want to explore. Of course, it is expected that teachers and students will find additional features worthy of attention, and the hope is that these ideas will provide a springboard for further study both around the concepts themselves and other similar texts. In particular, the focus on language as a system of choice would lend itself to re-creation, rewriting and substitution exercises to explore the effects of different kinds of constructions at various micro and macro levels (see for example Pope 1995).

The aim of this chapter then is to enable students to use a key concept from cognitive linguistics both to explore that concept in itself and use it in the service of detailed and systematic textual analysis. The activities that I suggest all involve the use of gesture, movement and the body as an important semiotic resource (actual embodied learning activities) and/or visual and diagrammatic representations (virtual embodied learning activities). As I have explained in previous chapters, these draw attention to the embodied nature of language, and allow students to experience those aspects through ways that draw on and utilise experiential basis of meaning. In doing so, it is hoped that the activities themselves will provide a vehicle for students to make implicit knowledge about language more explicit and consequently facilitate further debate and discussion in the classroom. For the teacher, I hope that the activities fulfil Halliday's notion of *grammatics*, in giving them a basis for using grammar (in its broadest sense here) as a tool for thinking with, and as a way of thinking about learning and teaching associated with linguistic study.

The remaining sections of this chapter are set out in the following way: each section's activities correspond to the concepts introduced in Chapter 5: figure and ground; modality; metaphor; deixis; clausal action chains; and imagined worlds. First, I explain the potential for each of these concepts to facilitate the exploration of texts using embodied learning activities, and provide some further information about any resources that are needed. I then suggest some initial activities that encourage students to explore language and grammar in an embodied way, followed by full details of an extended activity that centres on one text for each concept. Overall, the range of texts chosen is designed to fit in with texts that might usually be studied by Post 16 students around a variety of topics. So the range of texts includes a prose extract from the ghost story genre, charity promotional material, a 'conditions of use' document from a public organisation, political campaign material, a poem by a canonical English poet, newspaper reporting and advertising. However, there are no guidelines provided regarding timings, since in most cases, it would be impossible to do so, and teachers will naturally want to think of how much time they would want to allocate to parts of activities. In certain instances, photographs are included either to help teachers see the positions of students in certain activities, or to exemplify the embodiment of a particular language concept.

Since this chapter is more practical and therefore less theoretical than previous ones, there is no 'further reading' section offered. However, at the end of the chapter, suggestions are offered for further work based around the topic, either supplementary to or as an extension of the initial ideas and activities discussed. It is hoped that teachers will find these useful.

A note on terminology

The activities are all designed to encourage students to primarily explore the concepts behind aspects of grammar and meaning rather than learn a set of technical and abstruse terms. Where terminology is used, it is done so to provide a common language for the teacher to use in conjunction with the outlines for each section in Chapter 5. In many cases, I have left it up to the teacher to decide where and when terminology should be introduced and what this terminology should be. Clearly students need to know and be able to use linguistic terms accurately and convincingly, and this ability is to be encouraged. However, conceptual understanding should always come first, since this provides a genuine context and motivation for the assimilation of linguistic terms.

Figure and ground

The principle of figure and ground lends itself well to any embodied activity that stresses the physical nature of one element standing out against another as a fundamental principle of attention. Virtual embodied learning activities such as drawings that emphasise the figure–ground relationship within texts and parts of texts (for example within phrases, clauses and sentences) would be useful here. Equally, actual embodied learning activities that stress movement and the dynamic nature of figure–ground reconfiguration can encourage students to view the physical basis of the concepts of foregrounding in terms of parallelism and deviation.

Initial activities

The basic idea behind figure–ground can be explored by looking at visuals similar to that of Figure 5.1 (page 62). A more interesting approach would be to encourage students to see how the notion of figure–ground in texts is closely tied to our own perceptual systems, and particularly the way in which our visual system organises incoming stimuli to form a coherent and organised reflection of the world for us. This could be carried out in the following way.

Ask students to look at a static scene from a window (a field, car park, corridor, etc.) They should be able to identify something that for them 'stands out' as prominent (the figure) compared with the rest of the scene (the ground). They should be able to explain that the figure is usually brighter, more vivid or smaller than the ground. When movement is introduced into the scene (someone walking, a car being driven, etc.), attention is naturally diverted towards that moving entity, and consequently the figure–ground relationship is re-configured so that the moving object becomes the figure. This is usually quite straightforward to set up, although you may need to 'introduce' a moving object into the scene to demonstrate how this works. Alternatively, searching for 'car traffic' (or similar) on *YouTube* will return video footage that can be used in a similar way.

This principle can then be applied to short texts (poetry and advertisements are good for this) to show how the figure–ground principle operates as a way of assigning prominence. As I demonstrated in Chapter 5, this can be used in conjunction with the traditional notion of foregrounding.

Main text: extract from Susan Hill's novel *The Woman in Black*

Resources

Plain paper for drawing and storyboarding
Sheets of A4 paper labelled 'Eel Marsh House', 'narrator', 'door' and 'sound' for activity 2

The activities that follow on this text are designed to teach students the importance of foregrounding in written texts, and especially in prose fiction. As I explained in Chapter 4, foregrounding can manifest itself both in the establishing of textual patterns (phonological, lexical, semantic and syntactic) or through one of two kinds of deviation: internal deviation (the breaking away of a pattern from an established norm relative to that text) or external deviation (the breaking of a cultural, generic or semiotic norm). This extract can be used to teach both of these concepts using the cognitive linguistic notion of figure and ground. In each case, suggestions include both actual and virtual embodied learning activities in the form of movement, gesture and the use of visuals.

> This was the door without a keyhole, which I had been unable to open on my first visit to Eel Marsh House. I had no idea what was beyond it. Except the sound. It was coming from within that room, not very loud but just to hand, on the other

side of that single wooden partition. It was the sound of something bumping gently on the floor, in a rhythmic sort of way, a familiar sort of sound and yet one I still could not exactly place, a sound that seemed to belong to my past, to waken old, half-forgotten memories and associations deep within me, a sound that, in any other place, would not have made me afraid but would, I thought, have been curiously comforting, friendly.

But, at my feet, the dog Spider began to whine, a thin, pitiful, frightened moan, and to back away from the door a little and press against my legs. My throat felt constricted and dry and I had begun to shiver. There was something in that room and I could not get to it, nor would I dare to, if I were able. I told myself it was a rat or trapped bird, fallen down the chimney into the hearth and unable to get out again. But the sound was not that of some small panic-stricken creature. Bump bump. Pause. Bump bump. Pause. Bump bump. Bump bump. Bump bump.

(Hill 1998: 109)

Teaching ideas

One of the initial ways to explore foregrounding in the first paragraph is to ask students to sketch the situation being presented. This allows for a visual representation of what is being primed for our attention (i.e. placed as a figure) and relegated to the background (i.e. in position as the ground). This could be developed into a storyboard to allow students to consider how the scene is essentially a dynamic one, with the figure and ground configuration changing as the paragraph progresses. With each storyboard frame, students could comment on how elements are positioned as requiring attention and link these back to the textual properties that mark figures as perceptually salient. In this instance, presenting the information in a visual way should draw attention to the textual maintenance on the door ('this is the door…which…it'), and the subsequent reconfiguration of figure/ground when the sound becomes textually prominent and subsequently maintained over the rest of the paragraph. The pattern of internal deviation continues with attention drawn to the narrator's past, before a return to his current state and emotions at the end of the paragraph. Mapping out these shifts visually offers a way for students to understand the embodied nature of foregrounding.

To explore the embodied nature of figure and ground more explicitly, students can be assigned roles as one of the main entities in the first paragraph: Eel Marsh House, the narrator, the door and the sound. Students can then read through the text, physically positioning themselves in relation to each other, as either a textually prominent 'figure' or as backgrounded entities. As the paragraph progresses and these roles shift as outlined above, students move their position to express this textual pattern in an embodied manner (as in Figure 6.1). Towards the end of the paragraph, the sustained attention on the 'sound' has relegated other entities to the background. However, the final prominence given to the narrator, as shown in Figure 6.2, can be explored by students through the mapping of form to interpretation. Why in the context of a novel in the ghost genre, might the author want to divert attention to the narrator by the end of the paragraph?

Figure 6.1 Ongoing figure–ground configuration in an extract from *The Woman in Black*

Figure 6.2 Final figure–ground configuration in an extract from *The Woman In Black*

Students can explore the second paragraph of this extract in a similar way. Here, foregrounding occurs at the level of the sentence with a string of multi-clause sentences at the beginning of the extract followed by *minor* or *orthographic sentences* towards the end, 'Bump bump. Pause. Bump Bump...' Thus a figure–ground relationship is set up first in emphasising a range of action, with a number of figures given attention in the first sentences (students can demonstrate this pattern as in Figure 6.1) before the very specific and sustained attention that is afforded to the single noise at the end of the extract. There is therefore a figure–ground reconfiguration of clause patterns, and a prominence to that pattern shift (from many actions to a single action). In addition, the pattern of 'Bump bump. Pause. Bump bump. Pause.' is broken in the fifth orthographic sentence where the pauses stop and the final three sentences merely present the sound. The positioning of attention, initially equally distributed between sound and pause is now solely on the sound. In the context of the genre (a ghost story), students can explore and evaluate the interpretative significance of the final figure–ground configuration.

Further suggestions

- The activities detailed above could be used with any literary text where foregrounding of a particular character or theme is important. The matching of form to a particular interpretation demonstrates the significance of different kinds of textual patterns.
- This approach also works well with advertising, which often aims to foreground and emphasise a particular attribute, quality or idea about a product or company. Clusters of advertisements by the same company or based around the same product or theme would be good to explore, with students thinking about how different levels of language (graphology, lexis, syntax and so on) are given prominence. Using A4 paper as in Figure 6.1 and Figure 6.2 encourages students to think about the figure–ground configuration within their texts and provides them with a way of making patterns explicit: in advertisements for example, what tends to be figured, and at what level? And what tends to remain in the background?
- Presenting figure and ground in an embodied manner automatically involves using the body metaphorically to stand for another entity (e.g. sound or a door). Students could make further use of the body as a resource-making tool by exploring the relationship between entities that are part of a figure–ground configuration through movement and interaction. For example, how might each of the entities in Figure 6.1 be presented and shown to interact with each other using the body as the first paragraph progresses (e.g. Eel Marsh House as imposing and fearful, the sound as rhythmic and haunting and so on)?

Modality

Since studies in cognitive linguistics have emphasised the physical and force–dynamic basis of modalised constructions, modality as a phenomenon can be explored through embodied learning activities that draw on various notions of force. These include actual embodied learning activities such as kinegrams, and schematic and diagrammatic representations of types of force through virtual embodied learning activities. In the activities that follow I demonstrate how teachers can use some principles of force–dynamics in the classroom to encourage students to examine a complex conceptual and linguistic phenomenon.

Initial activities

Students can start by looking at the following utterances, all of which contain modal auxiliary verbs, together with a context in which each might occur or be spoken.

1   You **must** not enter the building before 9am [a teacher speaking to a group of students at school].
2   You **cannot** buy tickets on the train [a ticket inspector on a train talking to a passenger without a ticket].
3   You **may** open the window [a parent responding to a child's request].

In order to begin to understand the force–dynamic nature of these auxiliary verbs, students can first draw a sketch showing what they understand the central image or meaning of each of the utterances to be. This works best if students are asked to identify what for them is the main message or concept being promoted. The rationale for this is to get them thinking in non-linguistic imagistic terms so as to explore the kinds of force in modal constructions in a way that simply reading the utterances or saying them aloud with variations in tone could not hope to achieve. Figure 6.3 shows an example of two such sketches drawn by a student in response to utterance 1 (must not) and utterance 3 (may).

Using this as a starting point, the students should be able to explore how the modal auxiliary verbs 'must', 'can' (cannot) and 'may' in the utterances represent different kinds of force being transmitted between participants. In the two sketches shown, this force was interpreted as either blocking an action (utterance 1) or providing the means for one to take place (utterance 3). These were then directly linked to the contexts of the utterances, taking into account the degrees of inherent power attached to participants in each. These utterances could be supplemented by similar ones in a range of contexts to demonstrate that modal auxiliary verbs can be understood in the kind of image–schematic terms that were explained in Chapter 4. At this stage, they can also begin to investigate the different kinds of patterns that provide templates for the meanings of other modal auxiliary verbs: 'should', 'ought', 'could', 'might', 'will' and 'shall'.

With this underlying sense of patterns in place, students could then engage in a further activity to convey their thoughts on the conceptual content of each of these modal auxiliary verbs in the form of a kinegram, a precise embodied realisation of linguistic phenomena. This allows students to develop their initial ideas on image–schematic patterns to explore the embodied nature of meaning and the

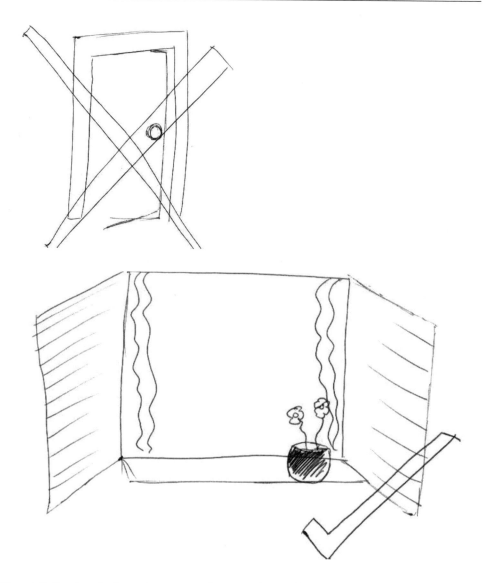

Figure 6.3 Sketches displaying the conceptual content derived from modal auxiliary verbs in
utterances 1 and 3

extension of a force schema based on physical movement into the more abstract
domains. In this way, the context of each of the utterances can also be 'played out'
through the ways in which the students interact with each other and use the physical
space of the classroom as a way of both demonstrating physical and psychological force
associated with each verb, and explaining its meaning. Examples of one set of students'
responses to each of the utterances are shown in Figures 6.4, 6.5 and 6.6.

Figure 6.4 Kinegrammatic interpretation of the conceptual content of 'must not'

Figure 6.5 Kinegrammatic interpretation of the conceptual content of 'cannot'

In Figure 6.4, the student's interpretation of the modal auxiliary verb 'must' in utterance 1 rests on her understanding of how the social and institutional power exerted by the teacher and school operates. In this example, the student uses pushing the classroom door as a way of showing how the restrictions imposed by the school are an extension of a type of force schema from the physical domain (a powerful entity blocking and preventing the ability of a less-powerful one from doing something). In Figure 6.5, a similar kind of power is understood in the ability of the company employee to impose a restriction. In this example, the students' interpretation incorporates a hand gesture that represents mental as well as physical blocking. And in Figure 6.6, the student's opening of her arm shows how the meaning of the modal

Figure 6.6 Kinegrammatic interpretation of the conceptual content of 'may'

auxiliary verb is this time underpinned by a sense of a restriction being lifted. In all of these examples, students are articulating meaning through exploring the embodied nature of modal constructions. And, since these exercises promote the view that grammatical structures are meaningful in their own right, they are able to understand language both as a repertoire of potential choices and as a principled and systematically organised way of representing experience arising out of and motivated by real situations of use.

Main texts: extract from 'Conditions of Use' document from The British Library, and an extract from a charity Christmas appeal by The Salvation Army (Figure 6.7).

Resources

Plain paper for sketches

31 **Laptop computers** may only be used in designated areas and must not be connected to the Library network.
32 Please turn **laptop sound off** before taking into a Reading Room.
33 **Headphones** can only be used if the sound is inaudible to other Readers.

If you send only <u>one</u> card this Christmas send this one

For many people, Christmas can be the most lonely time of all.

This card will be given to one of the many homeless or lonely people who count on us. Please help us prove that people really do care by signing the card and returning it with your gift.

If you do not want to put your name on the card, just sign it '**From a friend of The Salvation Army.**'

We will give your card to a homeless or lonely person. For many it may be the only reminder that someone cares.

You can rest assured that your address will not be disclosed with your Christmas message.

Figure 6.7 The Salvation Army Christmas campaign card

34 If the use of **personal equipment of any kind disturbs other Readers**, you will be asked to stop using it or to move to another desk.

35 **Portable storage devices or software must not be used** in conjunction with the Library's computers or electronic collections.

36 **The Library's electronic collections** may be viewed only on our designated computers. Under no circumstances may they be viewed on or downloaded onto your personal equipment.

37 The Library may **undertake safety checks of your technical equipment** at any time.

Extract from 'Conditions of Use of British Library Reading Rooms'.

Teaching ideas

Using a similar working practice to the utterances in the initial activities, students can explore the use of modalised constructions in these two texts. These offer particular types of text (a text outlining restrictions, and a text aiming to persuade and stressing the possibilities afforded by the charity receiving donations) that are likely to be read in both specific contexts and for very different reasons. These then provide good opportunities for students to examine the relationship between the choice of modal forms and contexts, and to think of the particular motivations for force-related patterns. Students should be encouraged to relate linguistic choice and form to contextual and generic influences and constraints. For example, they could explore

• How the use of deontic and epistemic modality varies according to the message the library wants to send (deontic when related to restrictions; epistemic forms when related to consequences of Readers not following conditions).

• The use of modal forms related to permission ('may') to emphasise the power the British Library holds over its Readers in being able to undertake certain actions and write these into its own terms of conditions. The balance between modal forms related to permission, certainty and obligation could be explored and commented on in interesting way using image–schematic sketches and/or kinegrams.

• The use of a variety of modal forms in The Salvation Army Christmas card, particularly those related to certainty and possibility, and how these forms relate to the purpose of the card to persuade people to support the charity.

• The use of politeness markers such as 'please' and imperative clauses, 'send this one' and 'help us prove' to support modal forms. Students can consider how these particular choices strengthen or mitigate modal force and why have they been used where they have.

Further suggestions

- Image–schematic sketches and kinegrams can be used to identify degrees of modal force along a continuum as explained in Chapter 5. For example, are there some modal constructions (and therefore texts), which present greater degrees of 'compulsion'? How can these be presented in an embodied way?
- The utterances and activities in this section only use modal auxiliary verbs. They could be repeated with examples and texts containing modal lexical verbs (e.g. 'permit') and modal adjectives/adverbs (e.g. 'possible' and 'possibly') to produce a more detailed analysis of the kinds of power inherent in modalised expressions in a text.
- Students could rewrite an extract using predominantly deontic, epistemic or boulomaic modal forms, and think about the effects of their writing, given the contexts and genres in which they would appear. For example, what happens to a sentence like 'I was in bed when I heard the doorbell ring' when it is rewritten with one type of modality dominating? 'I ought to have been in bed...', 'I was in bed – perhaps...', 'I wish I was in bed' and so on. How can they explain their choices and the effects of these in terms of physical and psychological notions of force?
- Students could collect and analyse other texts where modalised expressions occur with other features such as imperative sentences, politeness features and direct or indirect statements. They could explore how text producers make use of this range of language features to create particular effects. Working with extracts of political speeches and persuasive texts offers a range of possibilities for investigation.
- Charity advertisements offer very fertile ground for the study of modality since there is a need to strike a balance between urgency (strong modal force) and avoiding being too imposing (use of softer modal forms). They also provide a good opportunity to explore epistemic forms based on certainty or possibility where the force applied and understood is clearly more psychological than physical.
- Students could explore the idea of politeness in transcripts of speech by looking at why speakers might want to use more forceful or less forceful constructions as they interact. Asking students to articulate and reflect on choices through gesture and movement offers a good way of exploring the causes and effects of speakers' linguistic decisions.

Metaphor

In cognitive linguistic terms, metaphor involves the structuring and understanding of an abstract target domain through a concrete source domain via the process of mapping. Consequently, the body can be used to give a shape to, and explore the experiential basis of abstract entities that are represented through metaphorical constructions. Furthermore, since we tend to use gesture in everyday discourse as a way of activating and making explicit metaphorical constructions, the metaphorical nature of speech and writing can be explored through explicit attention being given to the process of *metaphor activation* (Müller 2008)

Initial activities

A good way to introduce students to the ubiquitous nature of metaphor would be to give them a short poem that contains a very clear use of metaphor ('The Sea' by RS Thomas would be a good example of this). Students should be able to identify and explain some of the more obvious metaphors and examples of similar tropes such as personification and simile. They could then be shown the extract from the political campaign flyer that I discussed in Chapter 5 on page 72, and asked to think about whether this text contains more, the same number of or fewer metaphors than the poem (depending on what you have chosen as the poem, it should roughly be around the same). This could lead to some discussion of whether metaphor is simply reserved for literary texts, and what the motivation for and impact of the metaphors used in the campaign flyer might be. At this stage, the discussion should be kept at this level and not be developed to explain more sophisticated terminology such as source and target domain, mapping and so on; students should be allowed to try to explain the process of metaphor in their own terms.

In a similar way, students can be introduced to the importance of gesture as part of the multimodal nature of communication. The best way to do this would be to ask students to video record a short conversation between two of their family members or friends, and watch this paying attention to the gestures speakers use and why they use them at particular moments during the discourse. They could also begin to try to explain and categorise any differences in the kinds of gestures that they are seeing being used. Having allowed students to explore and discuss this, the four dimensions of gesture (McNeill 2005) see page 49 could be presented to students so that they have a conceptual awareness of these distinct types. Any number of further activities related to spoken discourse and interaction could be developed from this. For example, the research by Goldwin-Meadow and Wagner (2005) on how gesturing decreases a speaker's cognitive load (see page 52) could provoke further work and discussion. What happens when speakers don't gesture? This could be investigated by asking speakers to converse without using any kind of gesture: do the research findings hold? Clearly this could form the basis of much more classroom discussion and work, including some potentially very interesting personal investigations.

Finally, students could draw metaphor and gesture together by looking at some explicit examples of metaphor and thinking about gestures that they might use when saying these. Alternatively, they could ask speakers to read them out, record and then comment on the kinds of gestures being used. Since these will largely be metaphorical gestures in McNeill's taxonomy, discussion should naturally lead to how gestures can support and even make explicit the metaphors they accompany. Depending on the class, teachers can choose whether to provide the term *metaphor activation*.

Main text: Conservative Party Campaign Poster from the 2010 General Election.

Resources

Paper and pens

Figure 6.8 Conservative Party campaign poster from the 2010 General Election

Teaching ideas

There are two ways in which students can explore the metaphors at work in this text and in doing so examine both the embodied nature of meaning and some of the typical characteristics of political discourse.

First, students can work in pairs reading through the text (or imagining it recast as a speech), exploring any gestures they think they would support particular words or phrases. In doing so, they are likely to attach specific gestures to metaphorical constructions that appear in the text. For ease of reference, these metaphors are listed below.

A COUNTRY IS A PERSON: 'A new government with the *energy, leadership and values*'; 'put the country back on *its feet*'.
UP IS GOOD: '*put* the country back on *its feet*'
THE ECONOMY IS AN OBJECT: 'get the economy *moving*'
POLITICS/POLITICAL CONCEPTS ARE PHYSICAL OBJECTS: '*clean up* politics'; '*sort out* our welfare system'; '*tackle* immigration'.
SMALL IS GOOD (BIG IS BAD): '*reduce* the deficit'
MOVEMENT/CHANGE IS GOOD: 'get the economy *moving*'; 'only the Conservatives can *bring the change Britain needs*'
REMAINING STATIC IS BAD: 'could *be stuck with five more years* of Gordon Brown'

For each of the gestures, students should try to explain how that gesture supports the meaning of the word or phrase, or in alternative terms, how it helps to create a vivid metaphorical construction. In doing this, they are both using a natural tendency that humans have to use gesture, and making metaphorical expressions more explicit and consequently open to further discussion, exploration and analysis. An understanding of the role of metaphor activation through gesture consequently leads to an opportunity to explore the embodied nature of abstract concepts in more detail.

This naturally leads to a second type of activity. The gestures used to activate metaphors will tend to be image–schematic. This is the case for example in the gesture in Figure 6.9, where the student was exploring how the metaphor THE ECONOMY IS AN OBJECT and its linguistic realisation 'get the economy moving' could be activated by a simple push gesture, here dependent on a SOURCE-PATH-GOAL schema (one entity moving along a line) and a FORCE schema (one entity being given energy and movement by another). However, an equally rich understanding and interpretation of the metaphors in this text can be explored through students using their bodies in more imaginative and comprehensive ways to explore how source to target domain mapping operates. Figure 6.10 shows one such demonstration. In this example, the students had decided to explore the linguistic metaphor 'sort out our welfare system', which is underpinned by the conceptual metaphor POLITICAL CONCEPTS ARE OBJECTS. To do so they considered the abstract notion of a welfare system in terms of something concrete, parts of a jigsaw that needed re-arranging so as to make a more coherent and organised whole. They clearly understood how this metaphor operated and the type of mapping from source domain (the world of objects and properties, and

Figure 6.9 Metaphor activation in 'get the economy moving'

Figure 6.10 Exploring the embodied nature of meaning and the experiential basis of 'sort out our welfare system'

in this specific case pieces of a jigsaw puzzle) and the target domain (the abstract notions of a political system and a part of that system). Indeed, their subsequent discussion centred on how their embodiment of that metaphorical expression not only helped them understand the experiential basis of the metaphor being used but also enriched their understanding of the text, the particular ideologies underpinning it, the political climate at the time of the 2010 election and the ways in which political discourse itself operated and would be received by voters. In other words, they were able to feed their work easily into a wider discussion of discourse, social and historical context and likely reception. At this stage, the teacher decided to build on the concepts they had experienced for themselves by introducing the notions of source domain, target domain and mapping. This type of approach, which is led by thinking and experiencing rather than the off-loading of terminology, is offered as a more effective way of teaching metaphor. To complete the detail on the exercise, the students were consequently able to explain cross-domain mapping as shown in Table 6.1.

Further suggestions

- The ideas explored in the section above could be applied to any number of political speeches, campaign advertising and journalism. Students could undertake an extended project to explore the prevalence and experiential basis of metaphor in these types of texts.
- Students can rewrite a text that relies on metaphor to make the source domain more upfront (for example, re-write the political campaign flyer as a football commentary). To what extent does this enable them to further understand some of the underlying principles behind both metaphor and the particular relationship between source and target domain? Are there any texts they can find that rely on this kind of *intertextuality*?
- Another excellent transformational task is for students to script and perform a written advertisement as a drama text to emphasise the embodied nature of abstract ideas. Students should ensure that they make the main metaphor the central focus

Table 6.1 Mappings in the conceptual metaphor POLITICAL CONCEPTS ARE OBJECTS

Source domain 'objects' (jigsaw puzzle)		Target domain 'political concepts' (welfare system)
Have physical properties	⟶	Have discrete parts (separate offices, ministers, workers, etc.)
Can be moved around	⟶	Can be moved from government to government
Can be improved or adapted in some way	⟶	Can be made better to improve people's lives
Can be organised	⟶	Can be restructured depending on a party's political ideology
Have an effect on people through interaction with them	⟶	Affect voters' lives

of their new text and think of physical/dramatic ways of exploring concepts. Alternatively, they could write a performance from scratch, choosing to present an abstract idea (love, friendship, economics, philosophy, etc.) through something physical. They could explore these either through gesture to look at the ways in which individual speakers activate metaphors, or through a similar focus to that exemplified in Figure 6.10.

Deixis

Since the notions of deixis, a deictic centre and deictic shifts are all understood as types of projection and movement, the best way to explore deixis in the classroom is through activities that encourage conceptual movement to be seen in physical terms. This can be in the form of actual or virtual embodied learning activities that reconfigure conceptual space as physical space either in the class or on the page. Clearly as space is important, it's best to undertake the following activities in a large classroom or hall, where students can explore deictic movement and projection in detail.

Initial activities

One of the easiest ways to encourage students to understand both the deictic nature of certain words, and the notions of a deictic centre, deictic projection and deictic shifting is to use an 'I here now' badge (easily made by writing the words 'I here now' across on a sheet of A4 paper) (see Figure 6.11). In pairs, it should be straightforward for students to understand how the referent of 'I' changes depending on who is wearing the badge (swapping the badge results in a perceptual deictic shift), and how the position in the classroom alters the referent of 'here' (here is always anchored to the position of the speaker at the time of utterance). In addition, they can explore the problematic notion of 'now' which with the passing of every second refers to a different set of temporal parameters.

This activity can be used to introduce perceptual, spatial and temporal deixis together with some associated deictic words such as pronouns, adverbs of place and adverbs of time. It can also show how deictic shifts necessarily represent a movement of some kind towards a new deictic centre, perceptually, spatially or temporally. To explore the effect of either a sustained movement or lack of movement in a literary text, students could explore the two passages from the openings to Chapters 1 and 4 of Ernest Hemingway's *A Farewell to Arms*.

A – In the late summer of that year we lived in a village that looked across the river and the plain to the mountains. In the bed of the river there were pebbles and boulders, dry and white in the sun, and the water was clear and swiftly moving and blue in the channels. Troops went by the house and down the road and the dust they raised powdered the leaves of the trees. The trunks of the trees too were dusty and the leaves fell early that year and we saw the troops marching along the road

Figure 6.11 'I, here, now' badge

and the dust rising and leaves, stirred by the breeze, falling and the soldiers marching and afterward the road bare and white except for the leaves.

B – The battery in the next garden woke me in the morning and I saw the sun
coming through the window and got out of bed. I went to the window and looked
out. The gravel paths were moist and the grass was wet with dew. The battery fired
twice and the air came each time like a blow and shook the window and made the
front of my pajamas flap. I could not see the guns but they were evidently firing
directly over us. It was a nuisance to have them here but it was a comfort that they
were no bigger. As I looked out at the garden I heard a motor truck starting on
the road. I dressed, went downstairs, had some coffee in the kitchen and went out
to the garage.

(Hemingway 1929: 1, 15)

Students can explore the deictic movement in these extracts simply by re-configuring
the classroom space into the fictional world brought to life in the text. Positioning
themselves from the deictic centre of the narrator, they can explore any shifts that occur
as the passages progress. In passage A, the deictic centre remains constant once the
parameters of the house 'in a village that looked across the river and the plain to the
mountains' are set up. In passage B, however, there is a continual sense of movement
from the initial deictic centre, marked by the deictic verb processes 'got out of' and

'went to', 'went downstairs' and 'went out'. All of these re-locate the deictic centre spatially. A more radical but still significant type of deictic shift can occur through a shift in relational deixis where a change in register is used. In this extract from Irvine Welsh's *Trainspotting*, the narrator Mark Renton switches from his local Scots dialect to Standard English (in bold) for a particular reason and with a particular effect. In this instance, the 'movement' is in the adopting of a different style of speaking and use of language in the service of making a particular point.

> When the auld man shot the craw, ah managed to cajole ma Ma intae gien us a couple ay her valium. She wis oan them fir siz months after davie died. The thing is, because she kicked them, she now regards hersel as an expert oan drug rehabilitation. This is smack, fir fuck's sake, mother dear.
>
> I am tae be under house arrest.
>
> The morning wisnae pleasant, but it wis a picnic compared tae the efternin. The auld man came back fae his fact-finding mission. Libraries, health-board establishments and social-work offices had been visited. **Research had been undertaken, advice had been sought, leaflets procured**.
>
> ...
>
> He wanted tae take us tae git tested fir HIV. Ah don't want tae go through aw that shite again....
>
> The auld girl sticks us in the comfy chair by the fire in front ay the telly, and puts a tray oan ma lap. Ah'm convulsing inside anyway, but the mince looks revolting.
>
> Ah've telt ye ah dinnae eat meat, ma, ah sais.
>
> Ye eywis liked yir mince n tatties. That's whair ye've gone wrong son, no eating the right things. Ye need meat.
>
> **Now there is apparently a causal link between heroin addiction and vegetarianism.**
>
> It's good steak mince. Ye'll eat it up, ma faither says. This is fuckin ridiculous. Ah thought there and then about making for the door, even though ah'm wearing a tracksuit and slippers. As if reading ma mind, the auld man produces a set ay keys.
>
> The door stays locked. Ah'm fitting a lock oan yir room as well.
>
> This is fucking fascism, ah sais, wi feelin.
>
> (Welsh 1993: 192)

Main text: 'Ozymandias' by Percy Bysshe Shelley.

Resources

Paper and pens

Ozymandias
I met a traveller from an antique land,
Who said – 'Two vast and trunkless legs of stone

Stand in the desert... Near them, on the sand,
Half sunk a shattered visage lies, whose frown,
And wrinkled lip, and sneer of cold command,
Tell that its sculptor well those passions read
Which yet survive, stamped on these lifeless things,
The hand that mocked them, and the heart that fed;
And on the pedestal, these words appear:
My name is Ozymandias, King of Kings,
Look on my Works, ye Mighty, and despair!
Nothing beside remains. Round the decay
Of that colossal Wreck, boundless and bare
The lone and level sands stretch far away.'

(Shelley 1977: 11)

Teaching ideas

Deixis can be used to explore the concept of poetic voice in this poem, demonstrating how the deictic shifts can be integrated into larger discussions of significance and meaning that can be attached to a poem that is popular at Key Stage 3, and has also appeared on GCSE and A level specifications. What follows offers some ideas for developing ideas on poetic voice using the notion of deixis. For an extended reading of the poem that draws heavily on deixis and deictic shift theory, teachers can also consult Stockwell (2002 and 2007).

Students can begin their exploration of the poem by considering a very simple shift that occurs at the initial of reading this text (or any other). Using the 'I here now' badge from the initial activities, they could discuss the first deictic shift that occurs in the act of entering the poem's 'world' and taking on the voice if the narrator. The first person pronoun 'I' that opens the poem thus positions the speaking voice in a different deictic centre (that of the narrator), probably requiring some kind of shift in time and space as well, depending on how the narrating voice is interpreted. Students could debate to what extent these shifts might take place. This initial positioning of the 'real reader' about to start reading the poem is demonstrated by a student in Figure 6.12. This focus on voice can be continued by asking students to mark any other perceptual deictic shifts they notice as they read through the poem, taking account of the triggers that initiate these shifts, and what new deictic centres they reveal. The best way to do this is to ask students to read the poem out loud in groups, acknowledging each perceptual deictic shift with a new speaker from the group. They should also use the space of the classroom to look at how each deictic shift projects into new conceptual space that is at a distance from the originating space. The shifts they identify ought to be something like this:

Voice 1: 'real reader'
Voice 2: 'the narrator' marked by the first person pronoun at the beginning of the
        poem

Figure 6.12 A real reader and 'Ozymandias'

Voice 3: 'the traveller', marked by the reporting clause 'who said'. This deictic centre also shifts temporally through the use of the past tense 'I *met*... who *said*', spatially through locations anchored by prepositions '*in* the desert', and '*on* the sand', and relationally in terms of the much more poetic register that marks the traveller's words

Voice 4: 'Ozymandias', marked through the direct speech that is placed on the inscription on the pedestal. The deictic centre also shifts temporally since Ozymandias speaks in the present tense. A further complexity is added by the fact that each of the previous 'voices' before this one also say these words in their reporting of another's speech

Voice 5: a shift back to either the traveller or the narrator (depending on how the poem is read). Most students will tend to interpret these words as being spoken by the traveller since the spatial parameters remain the same as those when the traveller first spoke, and the poetic register echoes that of the words before the deictic shift to Ozymandias in the middle of the poem

Figures 6.13a/b/c show a group of students working on the poem in this way. At each stage, a further deictic shift moves inwards and through the voices in the poem, marked by the 'I here now' badge moving progressively towards the left. Presenting the reading of the poem in a way that draws attention to movement enables students to explore the interpretative significance of these deictic shifts. Intriguingly, the default way of reading means that although the perceptual centre starts to shift back from the moment Ozymandias speaks, it remains located in the traveller, perceptually, spatially, temporally and relationally distant from the original narrating voice, and even more detached from our initial reading position as a real reader outside the world of the poem. Students can explore the significance of this pattern, drawing on the literary and historical contexts of a poem in a particular literary form and style (a sonnet) written by a nineteenth-century anti-establishment poet that explores the mutability and finiteness of human existence. The 'stranded' deictic centre offers a way of thinking about irony and shifting viewpoints in literary texts, and can yield some startling imaginative and sensitive responses. These will of course vary on the group undertaking the activities, but teachers might be interested in the following readings/interpretations/positions that have been offered when I have worked with students (from Year 7 right up to postgraduates) on the poem in this way.

- The poem as voyeurism (and the narrator/reader as voyeur): looking back on the past with both nostalgia but with a keenly felt sense of mortality, made stronger by the collapsing of poetic voice at the end of the poem.
- The poem as a cyclical process that mirrors the way we view history where voices move into other voices, where language itself burns brightly and then fades away.
- The poem as a reflection on the process of reading itself and the ways in which we 'push' ourselves deeper and deeper into fictional worlds when we read.
- The poem as a moral tale about the corrupt influence of rulers and a statement of Shelley's own political stance (the collapsed voices allows Shelley to adopt an ironic and indirect stance rather than criticise the establishment directly).

(a)

(b)

(c)

Figure 6.13 Perceptual, spatial and temporal deictic shifts in 'Ozymandias'

Further suggestions

- Students could develop their work on this poem by comparing it to Horace Smith's 'On a stupendous leg of granite, discovered standing by itself in the deserts of Egypt, with the inscription inserted below', written using the same stimulus as Shelley's poem (part of a statue of an Egyptian pharaoh Ramses II displayed at the British Museum). To what extent does Smith's poem address voice in the same way as Shelley's? Barlow (2009: 113–18) offers some further background information and ideas on comparing the two poems.
- Students can explore a selection of 'everyday' texts to identify the different types of deictic expression (perceptual, temporal, spatial, relational) and the ways in which readers are asked to adopt a particular deictic centre, which may shift through the act of reading. These can be mapped out as in Figure 6.13 or in diagrammatic form.
- More specific aspects of deixis can be explored in the following ways: use contrasting extracts (similar to the passages from *A Farewell to Arms*) to look at the effect of texts that initiate many deictic shifts and those that remain in one deictic centre; look at and explore the effects of a text that relies on shifts in register (social deixis); collect and categorise texts that rely on different types of deictic movement (e.g. travel guides, history textbooks, groups of text messages) – are particular deictic features linked to certain genres and text types?
- Use students' physical voices to explore deictic shifts in texts in a similar way to the activity on 'Ozymandias'. This works with any text but is particularly effective with poetry. Choose a poem that has shifts in any one of the four deictic areas and ask students to prepare a physical reading of the poem that utilises voice and physical movement to follow deictic shifts. Carol Ann Duffy's 'Beachcomber' is a good example of a poem that relies on a number of deictic shifts for its meaning and effects. Students could also explore any emerging patterns and dominant voices in poems that work in a similar way to 'Ozymandias'. Keats' 'La belle dame sans merci' is another example of a poem where the deictic centre remains 'stranded' at the end.
- Ask students to rewrite texts that rely on extensive use of particular deictic terms or on deictic shifts and consider the effect. For example, try re-writing a tourist audio-guide with no spatial deixis.
- Equally any text where the author's attitude is embedded within several different voices would be worth studying. Texts that shift between the present and past recollections or have competing voices (and by consequence deictic centres) from a variety of modes, genres, text types and registers (memoirs, reportage, witness reports and so on) would make excellent material for the classroom.

Clausal action chains

The notion of an action chain with the associated concept of energy transfer within a transitive clause that I outlined in Chapter 3 is best understood by students exploring the physical basis of such clause patterns. It provides an excellent way of teaching students about a crucial difference between the active and passive voice in terms of the prominence afforded to particular parts of the chain. The activities that follow focus on the use of the active and passive voice in a number of short examples, and in an extract from a newspaper report.

Initial activities

Students can work with the same set of clauses that were discussed in Chapters 4 and 5. These are reproduced below.

1   The man smashed the window with a stone
2   The man smashed the window
3   The window was smashed by the man
4   The stone smashed the window
5   The window smashed

In these examples, students can explore the concept of energy transmission and transfer by using plastic cups to demonstrate how in clause 1, this energy is transferred from an agent to a patient via an instrument. In Figure 6.14, the students demonstrate this by using the direction of the cups to show the flow of energy from the agent acting as its source through the instrument to the patient as the end of the chain, into which the energy is consumed. The resting point of the energy is shown by the use of the upside down cup. This pattern is repeated in Figures 6.15 and 6.16, where the students present embodied realisations of clauses 2 and 3, in each case the prominence afforded to

Figure 6.14 Energy transfer along a transitive clause (agent>instrument>patient)

Figure 6.15 Energy transfer realised in the active voice (agency focused)

Figure 6.16 Energy transfer realised in the passive voice (agency defocused)

either the agent (active voice) or the patient (passive voice) is demonstrated this time by one of the students physically identifying where the focus is in the clause. This exercise therefore enables students to explore the embodied nature of the transitive clause,

Figure 6.17 Energy resting point demonstrated in the clause 'The window smashed'

and the difference between the active and passive voice as one of focus and prominence rather than a simple transformation. Since prominence is always motivated by some external factor, this activity is a good introduction to the main activity for this section where students are asked to consider a text producer's likely motivation for a particular type of construal.

Finally, Figure 6.14 can also be used to explore clauses 4 and 5 with students. These (as with the other clauses) profile only a certain aspect of the entire process of transferring energy, and students can adapt the figure (either through acting or modifying a photograph or similar illustration) to show the profile and prominence afforded by these versions of the same scene. Clause 4 profiles only the instrument and the patient and downplays the agency behind the action while clause 5 no energy source or trail is specified, and the focus is simply on the end of the chain. The window is profiled simply as the resting point for the transmitted energy.

Main text: News report on fox attack

Resources

Plastic cups
String

15st man mugged by a fox

Beast's alley attack for food

By RACHEL DALE and FELIX ALLEN

BURLY Seb Baker told yesterday how he was mugged by a FOX — which nabbed garlic bread from his shopping.
The 15-stone civil servant was cornered after going to Tesco.

www.thesun.co.uk/sol/homepage/news/4179342/15st-man-mugged-by-a-fox-Beasts-alley-attack-for-food.html#ixzz2Ms9DG3lc

Teaching ideas

Once students have explored the difference between the active and passive voice in terms of the prominence afforded to different participants in the clausal action chain, they can explore the significance of the use of one form over another in a text. This short extract from a newspaper report at the height of a media frenzy about fox attacks in urban areas in March 2012 provides a good opportunity for exploring this.

The extract is intriguing because it shifts between various perspectives on the same scene (a fox taking garlic bread from a shopper). Given that this text is a newspaper report, there are clearly motivational and contextual reasons behind the choice of one form over another, for example, the need to appear to be entertaining, the typical sensationalism of the register of tabloid reporting and, of course, the desire to sell newspapers. It is important that students consider what these might be as they work on this text.

As with the examples of clauses in the initial activities, the different linguistic realisations represent the same process of energy transfer, with different aspects and participants being profiled at various times. As before, students can use plastic cups to present both the energy inherent in the action chain, and the prominence afforded to different parts of that process. Equally, a piece of string can act as an alternative way of showing energy flow and transmission from an agent to a patient.

Using the human energy chain, and using the profiles shown in Figures 6.14 to 6.17, students can draw attention to each of the focuses in the following forms, considering why in the light of the possible contextual factors related to production and reception, each has been used.

'15st man mugged by fox': passive voice with agency delayed.

'Beast's alley attack for food': the verb process here has been reified and so is presented in a nominalised form 'attack'.

'Burly Seb Baker told yesterday how he was mugged by a fox — which nabbed garlic bread from his shopping': reported form introduced by a reporting clause, agency delayed in passive voice but then followed by another clause in active voice that shifts prominence to the fox.

'The 15st civil servant was cornered': passive voice.

In discussing the above, students should be able to match linguistic form to contextual motivation with some idea of interpretative effect. The task also lends itself to some re-writing activities that enable students to explore the effects of choosing the active and passive voices in more detail. For example, students could think about what difference it would make if the extract read

A fox mugged a 15st man
A fox mugged burly Seb Baker yesterday who told us how it nabbed garlic bread from his shopping
The fox cornered the 15st civil servant

Following this, students could list a series of reasons why *The Sun* might want to present the man (emphasis on his weight, role of vulnerable victim) and the fox (given intention and 'human-like' agency ('jumped up' 'grabbed')) in this way? They could then re-write/re-present the article from an alternative perspective and one that sees the man and fox in alternative terms.

As an example, they might write from the point of view of

- Seb Baker
- A shopper who witnessed the event
- A spokesperson from the RSPCA
- The fox (!)

For each, they should consider both lexical and grammatical shifts that will need to be made. For example, Seb Baker would write in the first person 'I' and would be unlikely to describe himself as 'burly' (this sort of activity will should also give students further opportunity to explore the importance of genre and the register of tabloid reporting). These re-writings can be compared and contrasted with the original in terms of genre and motivation i.e. what sorts of things would each point of view want to place at the centre of the reader's attention, and which would they want to leave at the margins – and why. Students can also think about the attitude attached to particular lexical choices (for example 'beast', 'danger' and 'escape').

Further suggestions

- Students could find another series of headlines that draw attention to an event or experience through the use of varying patterns in the use of the active and passive voice. What motivation is there for presenting scenes and situations in a particular way through the profiling of certain parts of an action chain? Students can explore the ideological bases behind the representation of events, and the apportioning of blame to individuals and or groups. This would work well when used with a topic/event like the London riots or any coverage of political unrest, demonstration or war.

- Energy action chains can be further explored through examining the degrees of force behind verb choices. Based on the understanding that every choice made is at the exclusion of multiple other choices, students could explore the kinds of force different verb processes present, and any contextual and motivational reasons for their inclusion. This provides an excellent way of both exploring semantics and grammar, and integrating the textual and the contextual. For example, the following clauses all increase in the type of force each of the verbs suggests. How might these differences be shown in an action chain and how could students use these embodied realisations to explain the difference relationship between agent and patient in each?

I glanced at the letter>>I read the letter>>I scrutinised the letter

The police followed him>>The police shadowed him>> The police spied on him

Imagined worlds

As I demonstrated in Chapter 5, text world theory can be beneficial as way of looking at the contrast between states of affairs as a result of shifts in time, place or the introduction of modalised constructions that show belief, desire or obligation. The model can be a useful framework for teachers to consider when asking students to look at texts that project counterfactual worlds and presentations of events and people within them. Since the theory emphasises the text-driven nature of conceptualisation and its 'fleshing out' through encyclopaedic knowledge, it provides a particularly good model for using to analyse advertising, a genre that relies on presenting a contrast between the actual world and what that world could (and would) be like were the consumer to buy the product the company responsible for the advertisement is promoting.

Initial activities

A simple introduction to advertising would be to take the 'West Lodge Rural Centre' text (Figure 6.18) and ask students to explore the difference between their own discourse world (the actual world that as individuals they inhabit) and the text world that is set up by the advertisement. The advertisement is a good one to use since it simply presents a series of world-building elements that flesh out the world of the rural centre that it sets up for the reader.

In order to explore how the advertisement projects an alternative space, students could use a kinegram to show the conceptual leap into a new text world, and the stance that a reader takes up when engaging in reading an advertisement. Since advertising relies on readers making this kind of conceptual leap to imagine a different world to the current location, the use of a kinegram (an example of which is shown in Figure 6.19)

Figure 6.18 West Lodge Rural Centre advertisement

Figure 6.19 Using a kinegram to show the establishing of a new conceptual space (text world)

provides a way for students to begin exploring how this projected world is then developed in the course of reading the advertisement.

Students can now begin to explore this conceptual space or text world in more detail. Using text world theory's diagrammatic notation offers an easy way of allowing students to explore both how this projected world is built up, and how readers use their background knowledge to create a rich and fully formed understanding of exactly what this world will contain, and why it would be appealing to agree with the world the advertisement is projecting. Figure 6.20 shows one student's work on this text using a very simple diagrammatic notion as an example of a virtual embodied learning activity. In this instance, the notion and contents of conceptual space become embodied and explicitly set out on the physical page.

The template can be easily reproduced to allow students to examine their own understanding of how basic advertising operates in terms of projection and building on existing knowledge structures. In the top box (discourse world), this student has identified both the context of production (the advertiser's purpose and motivation) and the context of reception (her own influences and knowledge). This allows for a clear discussion of how meaning is a kind of negotiation between text producer and receiver. The

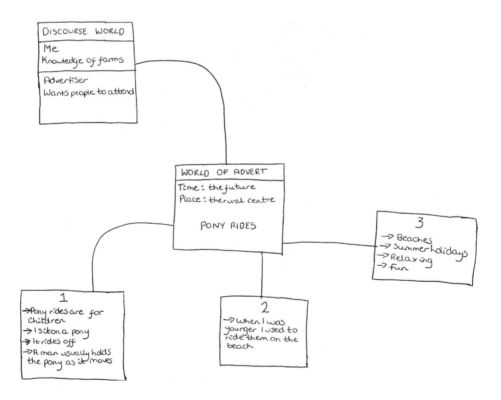

Figure 6.20 Diagrammatic presentation of world-building using text triggers and encyclopaedic knowledge in an advertisement

main box can be used to show how the world that the advertiser wants to portray becomes fleshed out as a rich conceptual space in the act of reading. The text projects a future time frame, where the reader is at the rural centre and engaged in the activities described in the advertisement. In this instance, the student has chosen one of these, 'pony rides', and begun to reflect on the kinds of knowledge that she relies on (and which the text producer to some extent will depend on her having) to transform this simple textual trigger into a rich meaningful and appealing element of the world of the rural centre. In this instance she has thought about the kinds of knowledge that she would use and begun to indicate this in the lower three boxes. In box 1, she has indicated how her knowledge of pony rides (they are primarily for children, the child sits on a pony, someone 'walks' the pony on a specified route and for a specified time) is important in her understanding of the kind of world the text producer is projecting (aiming for families). In box 2, she thinks about her own personal knowledge of pony rides when she was younger, and memories that they bring back. In box 3, she draws on more general knowledge about pony rides and any associated words, images and concepts that they bring to mind. Combined, her outlining of this encyclopaedic knowledge allows her to make explicit the implicit, and examine the automatic cognitive mechanisms that readers rely on when reading texts.

This approach allows students to explore how advertisements build on explicit textual features and degrees of encyclopaedic knowledge to build alternative spaces that are designed to be appealing. The example in Figure 6.20 uses only one entity in this text world, 'pony rides' but of course this could be extended to allow students to examine other named entities and attractions such as 'barrel rides', 'piglet racing', 'beautiful walks' and so on. Students can also compare their ideas to understand that although readers will tend to set up similar text worlds, there will always be some differences due to different kinds of knowledge, beliefs and memories being held by individuals. They can also be asked to consider how they might draw on different knowledge structures depending on where they read, with whom they read, and for what particular purpose they might be reading. Consequently, the use of this virtual embodied learning activity is a good way of showing the importance of the context of reception while not neglecting either the motivational factors behind the context of production or the importance of actual textual detail.

Main text: 'Karen's Blinds' advertisement

Resources

A3 paper for text world diagrams

For this activity, students can use a more complex advertisement (Figure 6.21) as a way of exploring the importance of knowledge structures, and to consider in more detail the way in which advertising projects a desired state of affairs that the reader is invited to 'flesh out' and contrast to their current state of being. In essence, advertising

Figure 6.21 Karen's Blinds advertisement

attempts to convince a reader that the world of the advertisement, involving a version of the reader affected in some positive way by the company's products would somehow be better than the current state of affairs in the discourse world, which is without the benefits of what the company has to offer and provide.

Students can approach this text in the same way as the 'West Lodge Rural Centre' advertisement, making use of diagrammatic notation to explore the combined effects of discourse world motivation, world-building textual detail and encyclopaedic knowledge in the shaping of meaning. However, this text is more complex, and there are a number of additional features that students could explore. Some of these are listed below with suggestions as to how identified features might impact on meaning, and how teachers might develop ideas from these in the classroom.

- The left hand side of the advertisement projects a world where the company visits 'your home' and measures 'your windows'. The focus on what the company as an attractive proposition will provide is emphasised in the syntactically and graphologically foregrounded first person plural pronoun 'We'. In this case, the projected text world contains a future version of the customer being given personalised customer service (marked through the repeated syntax of the possessive determiner 'your'+ noun structure) in the comfort of their own home.
- This side also projects a further temporal world-switch where within a period of seven days (assumed to be a golden target for advertisers), the blinds are fitted and consequently the customer can enjoy the benefits of his purchase. In turn, a further temporal world-switch asks the customer to imagine a period of twelve months following the purchase where the company will provide a guarantee, and by consequence (although not explicitly stated in the text), a further hypothetical world-switch where the blinds become faulty, and the company resolves the matter through its outstanding customer service.
- The right-hand side of the advertisement projects a world in which the customer has a vast range of choice (also graphologically foregrounded), and is consequently able to make exactly the purchase he is hoping for.
- In all of the above, the text producer is relying on the kinds of motivations and beliefs a potential customer will have with regards to making a purchase and valuing ways in which companies operate and promote customer service. Equally, the customer's encyclopaedic knowledge helps to flesh out this advertisement to present a projected situation: the customer having received all of this high-quality service and support, and now enjoying the benefits of making the purchase of the blinds. If successful, the appeal of projected state, and its contrast to the current state of affairs in the discourse world will mean that the customer feels positive about making a purchase from the company.

Further suggestions

- The approaches and activities described above would work well with any kind of advertising texts, as well as any other genres and text types that project or present a more desirable state of affairs, for example, political speeches, holiday brochures and so on.
- The activities and the text world theory model offer a very insightful way of exploring how different readers respond to the same text in different ways. Students could map out their own encyclopaedic knowledge that they feel is being triggered by textual detail in the construction of a particular text world and look at how this manifests itself in an idiosyncratic reading. Very common nouns such as 'house' and 'school' can of course have very different associative memories and knowledge structures attached to them, and students can explore how such structures subtly (or not so subtly) inform interpretation, and how text producers might play and rely on this. This is a good way of examining the importance of reader background knowledge on the act of reading, and might yield some interesting personal investigations.
- The activities are also a good way of drawing together the contexts of production and reception into a coherent whole, and thinking about how the meaning is always a form of negotiation between producer and receiver. Although these activities haven't examined spoken discourse, transcripts of conversations that students have collected could be used to explore how this kind of co-construction of meaning that is dependent on context and shared knowledge occurs.

Conclusion

In this chapter, I hope to have shown the potential for teachers to use the principles and concepts that I have introduced and discussed throughout this book to set up meaningful learning experiences for students that draw on the notion of embodied cognition. I have proposed a teaching methodology that utilises a range of teaching approaches involving the body, role-play, gesture and spatial and visual representation. As I have argued throughout previous chapters, I believe that a language pedagogy based on the premise that learning sequences should mirror cognitive ones, offers the teacher ways of encouraging and developing students' understanding of aspects of grammar, structure and meaning. It also provides resources for students to demonstrate the explicit externalisation of that understanding through analytical responses.

Chapter 7

Conclusion

In the introduction to this book, I argued that descriptive linguistics had the potential to be what I termed 'the great leveller', a way of redistributing analytical resources so that all students regardless of age or prior attainment can make purposeful, insightful and meaningful comments about language use in a range of different forms and contexts. Throughout the remainder of the book, I have also argued for the benefits of embodied learning activities, which build on cognitive linguistic principles, as an alternative to traditional models of teaching. I believe that these can offer a more enabling way for students to explore language and grammar. In this final chapter, I would like summarise my key points in the form of an alternative 'manifesto for grammar teaching' before offering some final questions for practitioners to reflect on.

An embodied learning manifesto for teaching language and grammar

The seven principles detailed below together represent what I believe are the main messages of this book, and together offer a vision for teaching language and grammar through embodied learning. In the context of a history of government initiatives and frameworks, and the continued influence of the assessment straightjacket and school accountability, there has never been a more interesting or important time to consider the place of language and grammar work in the English curriculum. The relationship between these external factors and what goes on in the classroom is necessarily complex not least because in varying degrees it is the teacher herself who gives a shape and an identity to the subject in her classroom. The ways in which she makes *English* 'pedagogically legitimate' (Menck 1995: 370) can to some extent be as forward thinking as she wants it to be, but is always bound within the context of a set of ideologies she holds regarding the nature of the subject. And ultimately, of course, real impact in the classroom happens not because of policy documents or government mandates, but because of the opportunities teachers give to their students.

1   Language is an important and worthwhile topic of study in the English curriculum – and not just in terms of developing skills.
2   Grammar should be taught explicitly but in contextualised and meaningful ways.

3 Pedagogies employed by teachers should be concept led, and avoid starting with lists of terminology that make it difficult for students to experience how language works in their own terms.

4 Due attention should be paid to terminology as a way of providing a shared and enabling metalanguage once the concepts they define have been internalised by students.

5 As teachers, we should always be open and responsive to, and indeed critical of, emerging research in education and the learning sciences with a view to how that might influence our teaching, and the students in our classrooms.

6 We should look towards advances in models of linguistics that complement what we know about the mind and the ways in which people learn, and acquire and use knowledge.

7 We should promote and celebrate the use of actual and virtual embodied learning as important semiotic resources in the English classroom.

This book finishes by asking teachers to think about some questions that I believe are worth further exploration given the scope and coverage of this book. There are no 'answers' to these as such; instead, I invite practitioners to view them as a series of starting points that will lead to reflective debate about the future possibilities for language pedagogy that I have raised.

Questions for practitioners

1 How might the classroom be best organised to promote and support embodied learning?

2 How might the ideas in this book be used more broadly within the English department, for example, in thinking about text choices on specifications, and designing programmes of study and schemes of work?

3 How might the ideas in this book be used across the post-16 curriculum as a way of developing students' cross-curricular skills?

4 How can teachers use the ideas in this book as a way of developing students' reading and writing skills more generally?

5 Beyond my suggestions in this book, what advantages does a cognitive linguistic approach have over other models of language study?

6 What potential barriers to implementing and using these ideas are there? How might these be overcome?

References

Abrahams, I. and Braund, M. (2012) (eds) *Performing Science: Teaching Chemistry, Physics and Biology Through Drama*, London: Continuum.

Ackerman, J., Nocera, C. and Bargh, J. (2010) 'Incidental Haptic Sensations Influence Social Judgments and Decisions', *Science*, 328: 1712–15.

Ainsworth, S., Prain, V. and Tytler, R. (2011) 'Drawing to learn in Science', *Science*, 333: 1096–7.

Andrews, R., Torgerson, S., Beverton, A., Freeman, T., Lock, G., Low, G., Robinson, A. and Zhu, D. (2006) 'The effect of grammar teaching on writing development', *British Education Research Journal*, 32(1): 39–55.

Arnold, M. (1932) *Culture and Anarchy*, London: Cambridge University Press.

Bain, R. (1991) *Reflections: Talking About Language*, London: Hodder and Stoughton.

Barlow, A. (2009) *World and Time: Teaching Literature in Context*, Cambridge: Cambridge University Press.

Bate, J. (1997) *The Genius of Shakespeare*, London: Picador.

Berry, M. (2013) 'Contentful and content light subject themes in informal spoken English and formal written English', in G. O'Grady, T. Bartlett and L. Fontaine (eds) *Choice in Language: Applications in Text Analysis*, Sheffield: Equinox, pp. 243–68.

Blake, J. and Shortis, T. (2010) *Who's Prepared to Teach School English?: The Degree Level Qualifications and Preparedness of Initial Teacher Trainees in English*, London: Committee for Linguistics in Education.

Bluett, J., Cockcroft, S., Harris, A., Hodgson, J. and Snapper, G. (2004) *Text: Message: the Future of A level English*, Sheffield: National Association for the Teaching of English.

Board of Education (1921) *The Teaching of English in England* (The Newbolt Report), London: HMSO.

Borg, S. (2003) 'Teacher cognition in grammar teaching: a literature review', *Language Awareness*, 12(2): 96–108.

Boroditsky, L. and Ramscar, M. (2002) 'The role of body and mind in abstract thought', *Psychological Science*, 13(2): 185–9.

Broaders, S., Cook, S., Mitchell, Z. and Goldwin-Meadow, S. (2007) 'Making children gesture brings out implicit knowledge and leads to learning', *Journal of Experimental Psychology*, 136(4): 271–88.

Bruner, J. (1983) *Child's Talk: Learning to Use Language*, New York: W. W. Norton.

Browning, R. (2000) *Selected Poems*, London: Penguin.

Burns, A. and Knox, J. (2005) 'Realisation(s): systemic functional linguistics and the language classroom' in N. Bartels (ed.), *Applied Linguistics and Language Teacher Education*, New York: Springer, pp. 235–326.

Cajkler, W. (2004) 'How a dead butler was killed: the way English national strategies maim grammatical parts', *Language and Education*, 18(1): 1–16.

Cajkler, W. and Hislam, J. (2002) 'Trainee teachers' grammatical knowledge: the tension between public expectation and individual competence', *Language Awareness*, 11(3): 161–77.

Carter, R. (1982) *Linguistics and the Teacher*, London: Routledge.

Carter, R. (1990) 'Introduction' in R. Carter (ed.) *Knowledge about Language and the Curriculum: The LINC Reader*, London: Hodder and Stoughton, pp. 1–20.

Carter, R. (1996) 'Politics and knowledge about language: the LINC project' in G. Williams and R. Hasan (eds) *Literacy in Society*, Harlow: Longman, pp. 1–28.

Carter, R. (2004) *Language and Creativity: The Art of Common Talk*, London: Routledge.

Carter, R. and Stockwell, P. (2008) *The Language and Literature Reader*, London: Routledge.

Cawley, F. (1958) The difficulty of English grammar for students of secondary school age', *British Journal of Educational Psychology*, 28: 174–6.

Chomsky, N. (1957) *Syntactic Structures*, Berlin: De Gruyter.

Chomsky, N. (1998) *On Language*, New York: The New Press.

Clark, B. and Owtram, N. (2012) 'Imagined inference: teaching writers to think like readers' in M. Burke, S. Csábi, L. Week and J. Zerkowitz (eds) *Pedagogical Stylistics: Current Trends in Language, Literature and ELT*, London: Bloomsbury, pp. 126–41.

Clark, U. (2010) 'The problematics of prescribing grammatical knowledge: the case in England' in T. Locke (ed.) *Beyond the Grammar Wars: A Resource for Teachers and Students on Developing Language Knowledge in the English/Literacy Classroom*, London: Routledge, pp. 38–54.

Close, E., Close, H., McKagan, S. and Scherr, R. (2010) 'Energy in action: the construction of physics ideas in multiple modes', *2010 Physics Education Research Conference Proceedings*, 1289: 105–8.

Collerson, J. (1997) *Grammar in Teaching*, Newtown, New South Wales: Primary English Teaching Association.

Corballis, M. (2002) *From Hand to Mouth: The Origins of Language*, Princeton, NJ: Princeton University Press.

Corballis, M. (2012) 'How language evolved from manual gestures', *Gesture*, 12(2): 200–26.

Creek, P. (1967) 'Language study for the sixth form', in J. Britton (ed.) *Handbook for English Teachers: 2 Talking and Writing*, London: Methuen, pp. 91–9.

Crystal, D. (2010) *The Cambridge Encyclopaedia of Language*, 3rd edn., Cambridge: Cambridge University Press.

Dean, G. (2003) *Grammar for Improving Writing and Reading in the Secondary School*, London: David Fulton.

DES (1964) *The Examining of English Language: Eighth Report of the Secondary School Examinations Council*, London: HMSO.

DES (1975) *A Language for Life* (The Bullock Report), London: HMSO.

DES (1984) *English from 5–16, Curriculum Matters 1*, London: HMSO.

DES (1986) *English from 5–16, Curriculum Matters 1, Second Edition (Incorporating Responses)*, London: HMSO.

DES (1988) *Report of the Committee of Inquiry into The Teaching of English Language* (The Kingman Report), London: HMSO.

DESWO (1989) *English 5–16* (The Cox Report), London: HMSO.

DfE (2011) *Independent Review of Key Stage 2 Testing, Assessment and Accountability* (The Bew Report), London: DfE.

DfE (2013a) *English Programmes of Study: Key Stages 1 and 2: National Curriculum in England*, London: DfE.

DfE (2013b) *English Programmes of Study: Key Stage 3: National Curriculum in England*, London: DfE.

DfE (2013c) *English Language: GCSE Subject Content and Assessment Objectives*, London: DfE.

Doležel, L. (1998) *Heterocosmica – Fiction and Possible Worlds*, Baltimore, MD: Johns Hopkins University Press.

Doughty, P., Pearce, J. and Thornton, G. (1971) *Language in Use*, London: Edward Arnold.

Eaglestone, R. (2002) *Doing English: A Guide for Literature Students*, London: Routledge.

Eggar, T. (1991) 'Correct use of English is essential', *Times Educational Supplement*, 28 June.

Elley, W., Barham, I., Lamb, H. and Wyllie, M. (1979) *The Role of Grammar in a Secondary School Curriculum*, Wellington: New Zealand Council for Educational Research.

Ellis, V. and Briggs, J. (2011) 'Teacher education and applied linguistics: what needs to be understood about what, how and where beginning teachers learn', in S. Ellis and E. McCartney (eds) *Applied Linguistics and Primary School Teaching*, Cambridge: Cambridge University Press, pp. 276–89.

Evans, V. and Green, M. (2006) *Cognitive Linguistics: An Introduction*, Edinburgh: Edinburgh University Press.

Fairclough, N. (2002) *Language and Power*, London: Longman.

Fleming, M. (2011) *Starting Drama Teaching*, London: Routledge.

Franks, A. and Jewitt, C. (2001) 'The meaning of action in learning and teaching', *British Educational Research Journal*, 27(2): 201–17.

French, R. (2010) 'Primary school children learning grammar: rethinking the possibilities', in T. Locke (ed.) *Beyond the Grammar Wars: A Resource for Teachers and Students on Developing Language Knowledge in the English/Literacy Classroom*, London: Routledge, pp. 206–29.

Gallagher, S. (2005) *How the Body Shapes the Mind*, New York: Oxford University Press.

Gallese, V. and Goldman, A (1998) 'Mirror neurons and the simulation theory of mind reading', *Trends in Cognitive Science*, 2(12): 493–501.

Gavins, J. (2007) *Text World Theory: An Introduction*, Edinburgh: Edinburgh University Press.

Geary, J. (2012) *I Is An Other: The Secret Life of Metaphor and How it Shapes the Way We See the World*, New York: HarperCollins.

Gibbons, S. (2013) *The London Association for the Teaching of English 1947–67: A History*, London: Trentham Books.

Gillard, D. (2011) *Education in England: A Brief History*. Available at: www.educationengland.org.uk/history (last accessed 4th January 2014).

Giovanelli, M. (2010) 'A text world theory approach to the teaching of poetry', *English in Education*, 44(3): 214–31.

Giovanelli, M. (2013) *Text World Theory and Keats' Poetry: The Cognitive Poetics of Desire, Dreams and Nightmares*, London: Bloomsbury.

Goddard, A. (1993) *Researching Language: English Project Work at A level and Beyond*, Dunstable: Folens.

Goddard, A. (2012) *Doing English Language: A Guide for Students*, London: Routledge.

Goddard, A. and Beard, A. (2007) *As simple as ABC?: Issues of Transition for Students of English Language A Level Going on to Study English Language /Linguistics in Higher Education*, London: Higher Education Academy/English Subject Centre.

Goldwin-Meadow, S. and Wagner, S. (2005) 'How our hands help us learn', *TRENDS in Cognitive Science*, 9(5): 234–41.

Halliday, M. (1967) 'Linguistics and the teaching of English' in J. Britton (ed) *Handbook for English Teachers: 2. Talking and Writing*, London: Methuen, pp. 80–90.

Halliday, M. (2002) 'On grammar and grammatics' in J. Webster (ed.) *On Grammar: Vol 1 of the Collected Works of M.A.K. Halliday*, London: Continuum: pp. 384–417.

Halliday, M. (2007) *Language and Education: Volume 9 in the Collected Works of M.A.K. Halliday*, London: Continuum.

Halliday, M. and Matthiesen, C. (2013) *Halliday's Introduction to Functional Grammar*, 4th edn., London: Routledge.

Hamblin, K. (1987) *Mime: A Playbook of Silent Fantasy*, Cambridge: Lutterworth Press.

Hancock, C. (2005) *Meaning-Centered Grammar: An Introductory Text*, London: Equinox.

Hancock, C. and Kolln, M. (2010) 'Blowin' in the wind: English grammar in United States schools', in T. Locke (ed.) *Beyond the Grammar Wars: A Resource for Teachers and Students on Developing Language Knowledge in the English/Literacy Classroom*, London: Routledge, pp. 21–37.

Harris, R. (1962) *An Experimental Enquiry into the Functions and Value of Formal Grammar in the Teaching of English, with Special Reference to the Teaching of Correct Written English to Children Aged Twelve to Fourteen*, Unpublished PhD thesis, University of London.

Hattie, J. and Yates, G. (2013) *Visible Learning and the Science of How We Learn*, London: Routledge.

Havránek, B. (1964) 'The functional differentiation of the standard language', in P. Garvin (ed.) *A Prague School Reader on Esthetics, Literary Structure and Style*, Georgetown, DC: Georgetown University Press.

Hawkins, E. (1984) *Awareness of Language: An Introduction*, 2nd edn., Cambridge: Cambridge University Press.

Hemingway, E. (1929) *A Farewell to Arms*, London: Jonathan Cape.

Hill, S. (1998) *The Woman in Black*, London: Vintage.

Hodge, R. and Kress, G. (1988) *Social Semiotics*, Cambridge: Polity Press.

Holme, R. (2009) *Cognitive Linguistics and Language Teaching*, Basingstoke: Palgrave Macmillan.

Holme, R. (2012) 'Cognitive linguistics and the second language classroom', *TESOL Quarterly*, 46(1): 6–29.

Hope, G. (2008) *Thinking and Learning Through Drawing in Primary Classrooms*, London: Sage Publications.

Hostetter, A. (2011) 'When do gestures communicate: a meta-analysis', *Psychological Bulletin*, 137(2): 297–315.

Hudson, R. and Walmsley, J. (2005) 'The English Patient: English grammar and teaching in the twentieth century', *Journal of Linguistics*, 43(3): 593–622.

Hughes, C. (1991) 'The teaching of English arouses strong arguments between 'tradition' and 'progress' ', *The Independent*, 11th July.

Iacoboni, M. (2008) *Mirroring People: The New Science of How We Connect With Others*, New York: Farrar, Straus and Giroux.

Johnson, M. (1987) *The Body in the Mind: the Bodily Basis of Meaning, Imagination and Reason*, Chicago, IL: Chicago University Press.

Keith, G. (1990) 'Language study at Key Stage 3', in R. Carter (ed.) *Knowledge about Language and the Curriculum: The LINC Reader*, London: Hodder and Stoughton, pp. 69–103.

Kolln, M. and Gray, L. (2012) *Rhetorical Grammar: Grammatical Choices, Rhetorical Effects*, 7th edn., New York: Longman.

Kövecses, Z. (2002) *Metaphor: A Practical Introduction*, New York: Oxford University Press.

Kress, G., Jewitt, C., Ogborn, J. and Tsatsarelis, C. (2001) *Multimodal Teaching and Learning: The Rhetorics of the Science Classroom*, London: Continuum.

Kureishi, H. (1998) *Intimacy*, London: Faber and Faber.

Lakoff, G. (1992) 'Metaphor and war: the metaphor system used to justify war in the Gulf', in H. Kreisler (ed.) *Confrontation in the Gulf: University of California Professors Talk About the War*, Berkeley, CA: Institute of International Studies.

Lakoff, G. and Johnson, M. (1980) *Metaphors We Live By*, Chicago, IL: University of Chicago Press.

Lakoff, G. and Johnson, M. (1999) *Philosophy in the Flesh: The Embodied Mind and Its Challenge to Western Thought*, New York: Basic Books.

Lakoff, G. and Turner, M. (1989) *More than Cool Reason: A Field Guide to Poetic Metaphor*, Chicago, IL: University of Chicago Press.

Langacker, R. (2008a) 'The relevance of cognitive grammar for language pedagogy', in S. De Knop and T. De Rycker (eds) *Cognitive Approaches to Pedagogical Grammar: A Volume in Honour of René Dirven*, New York: Mouton de Gruyter, pp. 7–36.

Langacker, R. (2008b) *Cognitive Grammar: A Basic Introduction*, New York: Oxford University Press.

Lapaire, J. (2006) *La Grammaire Anglaise en Mouvement*, Paris: Hachette.

Lapaire, J. (2007) 'The meaning of meaningless grams – or emptiness revisited', in W. Oleksy and P. Stalmaszczyk (eds) *Cognitive Approaches to Language and Linguistic Data*, Frankfurt: Peter Lang, pp. 241–58.

Leech, G. and Short, M. (2007) *Style In Fiction: A Linguistic Introduction to English Fictional Prose*, 2nd edn., Harlow: Pearson Education.

Littlemore, J. (2009) *Applying Cognitive Linguistics to Second Language Teaching and Learning*, Basingstoke: Palgrave Macmillan.

Locke, T. (2010) (ed.) *Beyond the Grammar Wars: A Resource for Teachers and Students on Developing Language Knowledge in the English/Literacy Classroom*, London: Routledge.

Macauley, W. (1947) 'The difficulty of grammar', *British Journal of Educational Psychology*, 18: 153–62.

Macken-Horarik, M. (2009) 'Navigational metalanguages for new territory in English; the potential of grammatics', *English Teaching: Practice and Critique*, 8(3): 55–69.

Macken-Horarik, M. (2012) 'Why school English needs a 'good enough' grammatics (and not more grammar)', *Changing English: Studies in Culture and Education*, 19(2): 179–94.

Mandler, J. (2004) *Foundations of Mind: Origins of Conceptual Thought*, New York: Oxford University Press.

Mathieson, M. (1975) *The Preachers of Culture: A Study of English and its Teachers*, London: George Allen and Unwin.

Matthews, J. (2003) *Drawing and Painting: Children and Visual Representation*, London: Sage Publications.

McEwan, I. (2007) *On Chesil Beach*, London: Jonathan Cape.

McNeill, D. (1985) 'So you think gestures are nonverbal?', *Psychological Review*, 92: 350–71.

McNeill, D. (2005) *Gesture and Thought*, Chicago, IL: University of Chicago Press.

Menck, P. (1995) 'Didactics as construction of content', *Journal of Curriculum Studies*, 27(4): 353–71.

Ministry of Education (1963) *Half Our Future* (The Newsom Report), London: HMSO.

Moll, L., Amanti, C., Neff, D. and Gonzalez, N. (1982) 'Funds of knowledge for teaching: using a qualitative approach to connect homes and classrooms', *Theory Into Practice*, 31(2): 132–41.

Mount, H. (2013) 'If you don't know grammar, you can't write English', *The Telegraph*. Avaiable at: http://blogs.telegraph.co.uk/culture/harrymount/100068896/if-you-dont-know-grammar-you-cant-write-english/ (last accessed 23rd January 2014).

Müller, C. (2008) *Metaphors Dead and Alive, Sleeping and Waking: A Dynamic View*, Chicago, IL: University of Chicago Press.

Myhill, D. (2000) 'Misconceptions and difficulties in the acquisition of metalinguistic knowledge', *Language and Education*, 14(3): 151–63.

Myhill, D. (2011) 'Grammar for designers: how grammar supports the development of writing', in S. Ellis and E. McCartney (eds) *Applied Linguistics and Primary School Teaching*, Cambridge: Cambridge University Press, pp. 81–92.

Myhill, D., Jones, S., Lines, H. and Watson, A. (2012) 'Re-thinking grammar: the impact of embedded grammar teaching on students' writing and students' metalinguistic understanding', *Research Papers in Education*, 27(2): 139–66.

Myhill, D., Jones, S., Watson, A. and Lines, H. (2013) 'Playful explicitness with grammar: a pedagogy for writing', *Literacy*, 47(2): 103–11.

Nicholls, B. (1975) *Move: A Practical Handbook for Teachers Introducing Drama and Movement into Secondary Schools*, London: Heinemann.

Palmer, F. (2001) *Mood and Modality*, 2nd edn., Cambridge: Cambridge University Press.

Pope, R. (1995) *Textual Intervention: Critical and Creative Strategies for Literary Studies*, London: Routledge.

Poulson, L. (1998) *The English Curriculum in Schools*, London: Cassell.

Poulson, L., Radnor, H. and Turner-Bisset, R. (1996) 'From policy to practice: language education, English teaching and curriculum reform in secondary schools in England', *Language and Education*, 10(1): 33–46.

QCA (1998) *The Grammar Papers: Perspectives on the Teaching of Grammar in the National Curriculum*, London: QCA Publications.

QCA (1999) *Not Whether But How: Teaching Grammar in English at Key Stages 3 and 4*, London: QCA Publications.

Quirk, R. (1962) *The Use of English*, London: Longman.

Rapeer, L. (1913) 'The problem of formal grammar in elementary education', *The Journal of Educational Psychology*, 4(3): 125–37.

Richmond, J. (1992) 'Unstable materials: the LINC story', *The English and Media Magazine*, 26: 13–18.

Ridout, R. (1947) *English Today 1*, London: Ginn and Company.

Rose, D. and Martin, J. (2012) *Learning to Write, Reading to Learn: Genre, Knowledge and Pedagogy in the Sydney School*, London: Equinox.

Scherr, R., Close, H., McKagan, S. and Close, E. (2010) ' 'Energy theater': using the body symbolically to understand energy', *2010 Physics Education Research Conference Proceedings*, 1289: 293–6.

Scott, P. (1989) *Reconstructing A Level English*, Milton Keynes: Open University Press.

Sealey, A. (1994) 'Language and educational control: the construction of the LINC controversy', in D. Scott (ed.) *Accountability and Control in Educational Settings*, London: Cassell.

Segal, E.M. (1995) 'Narrative comprehension and the role of deictic shift theory', in J.F. Duchan, G.A. Bruder and L.E. Hewitt (eds) *Deixis in Narrative: A Cognitive Science Perspective*, Hillsdale, NJ: Lawrence Erlbaum, pp. 3–17.

Semino, E. (2008) *Metaphor and Discourse*, Cambridge: Cambridge University Press.

Shelley, P. (1977) *Selected Poems*, London: J. M. Dent.

Shulman, L. (1986) 'Those who understand: knowledge growth in teaching', *Educational Researcher*, 15(2): 4–14.

Shuttleworth, J. (1988) 'On Advanced Level English Language', in M. Jones and A. West (eds) *Learning Me Your Language: Perspectives on the Teaching of English*, London: Mary Glasgow, pp. 148–53.

Simpson, P. (2014) *Stylistics: A Resource Book for Students*, 2nd edn. London: Routledge.

Stamenov, M. (2002) 'Some features that make mirror neurons and the human language faculty unique', in M. Stamenov and V. Gallese (eds) *Mirror Neurons and the Evolution of Brain and Language*, Amsterdam: John Benjamins, pp. 249–72.

Stockwell, P. (2002) *Cognitive Poetics: An Introduction*, London: Routledge.

Stockwell, P. (2007) 'On teaching literature itself', in G. Watson and S. Zyngier (eds) *Literature and Stylistics for Language Learners: Theory and Practice*, Basingstoke: Palgrave Macmillan, pp. 15–26.

Stockwell, P. (2009) *Texture: A Cognitive Aesthetics of Reading*, Edinburgh: Edinburgh University Press.

Sweetman, J. (1991) 'Missing Link – Curriculingo', *The Guardian*, 19 October.

Sweetser, E. (1990) *From Etymology to Pragmatics: Metaphorical and Cultural Aspects of Semantic Structure*, Cambridge: Cambridge University Press.

Talmy, L. (1988) 'Force dynamics in language and cognition', *Cognitive Science*, 12, 49–100.

Thompson, G. (2013) *Introducing Functional Grammar*, 3rd edn., London: Routledge.

Tinkel, T. (1988) *Explorations in Language*, Cambridge: Cambridge University Press.

Tomasello, M., Carpenter, M. and Liszkowski, U. (2007) 'A new look at infant pointing', *Child Development*, 78(3): 705–22.

Tomlinson, D. (1994) 'Errors in the Research into the Effectiveness of Grammar Teaching', *English in Education*, 28(1): 20–6.

Tyler, A. (2012) *Cognitive Linguistics and Second Language Learning: Theoretical Basics and Experimental Evidence*, London: Routledge.

Ungerer, F. and Schmid, H. (2006) *An Introduction to Cognitive Linguistics*, London: Longman.

Unsworth, L. (2005) (ed.) *Researching Language in Schools and Communities: Functional Linguistic Perspectives*, London: Continuum.

Vygotsky, L. (1986) *Thought and Language*, 2nd edn., Cambridge, MA: MIT Press.

Vygotsky, L.S. (1987) *The Collected Works of L. S. Vygotsky, Volume 1: Problems of General Psychology*, New York: Plenum Press.

Walden, G. (1991) 'Why the government must expel the unteachable elite', *Daily Telegraph*, 3rd July.

Wales, L. (2009) 'Reviving the dead butler: towards a review of national literacy strategy grammatical advice', *Language and Education*, 23(6): 523–40.

Wall, K, Higgins, S. and Smith, H. (2005) ' 'The visual helps me understand the complicated things': pupil views of teaching and learning with interactive whiteboards', *British Journal of Educational Technology*, 36: (5), 851–67.

Walmsley, J. (1984) 'The uselessness of formal grammar', *CLIE Pamphlet 2*, London: Committee for Linguistics in Education.

Watson, H. (2012) 'Navigating 'the pit of doom': affective responses to teaching 'grammar' ', *English in Education*, 46(1): 21–36.

Welsh, I. (1993) *Trainspotting*, London: Secker and Warburg.

Werth, P. (1999) *Text Worlds: Representing Conceptual Space in Discourse*, London: Longman.

Williams, G. (1998) 'Children entering literate worlds: perspectives from the study of textual practices', in F. Christie and R. Misson (eds) *Literacy and Schooling: New Challenges, New Possibilities*, London: Routledge, pp.18–46.

Williamson, J. and Hardman, F. (1995) 'Time for refilling the bath? A study of primary student teachers' grammatical knowledge', *Language and Education*, 9(2): 117–34.

Willingham, D. (2010) *Why Don't Students Like School? A Cognitive Scientist Answers Questions about how the Mind Works and What it Means for the Classroom*, San Francisco, CA: Jossey-Bass.

Wilson, S., Saygin, A., Sereno, M. and Iacoboni, M. (2004) 'Listening to speech activates motor areas involved in speech production', *Nature Neuroscience*, 7: 701–2.

Wyse, D. (2001) 'Grammar for writing? A critical review of empirical evidence', *British Journal of Educational Studies*, 49: 411–27.

Wyse, D., Jones, R., Bradford, H. and Wolpert, M. (2013) 'Grammar', in *Teaching English Language and Literacy*, 3rd edn., London: Routledge, pp. 257–66.

Index